Leo Tolstoy

The Physiology of War

Napoleon and the Russian campaign

Leo Tolstoy

The Physiology of War
Napoleon and the Russian campaign

ISBN/EAN: 9783337309848

Printed in Europe, USA, Canada, Australia, Japan

Cover: Foto ©Thomas Meinert / pixelio.de

More available books at **www.hansebooks.com**

THE PHYSIOLOGY OF WAR

NAPOLEON

AND

THE RUSSIAN CAMPAIGN

BY

COUNT LEO TOLSTOÏ

TRANSLATED FROM THE THIRD FRENCH EDITION

BY

HUNTINGTON SMITH

NEW YORK

THOMAS Y. CROWELL & CO.

No. 13 Astor Place

CONTENTS.

TRANSLATOR'S PREFACE.

———

IT is now three years since the writer of this introduction had the pleasure of bringing before American readers that curiously interesting book by Count Leo Tolstoï, " My Religion," a work which, perhaps more than any other production of its author, has excited wide speculation and discussion. Up to that time Count Tolstoï was practically unknown to readers this side the Atlantic. His name was unfamiliar, the details of his remarkable life were not accessible in any dictionary of biography. In three years, what a change !

Now no less than fourteen of his works have been translated and published in this country ; the minutest particulars concerning his personality, his opinions, and his mode of life are reported with the utmost fidelity. His grand, brooding, sympathetic countenance is familiar to the very loiterers by the news-venders' windows. He is known by many eager, searching minds to be the one colossal figure in contem- porary literature.

What has led to this significant and rapid increase of popular esteem? It was felt at once that Count Tolstoï had a message to de- liver, a message worth hearing, and the world has shown itself ready to hear. The utter- ance of this message began in his earliest writings, and it has gone on, swelling in vol- ume and power with each succeeding produc- tion of his pen. As we look back now in the light of later revelation, we can see the thread of ethical purpose running through all his writ- ings, growing more and more plain with each one of them, and at length woven into a com- plete pattern in the book which is his most characteristic, because his most outspoken work, the book which reveals most clearly his own mental attitude toward his fellows, and his conception of man's part in the universe.

The message may be summed up very briefly; it expresses the essential dignity of manhood, and declares the most crying need in the world to-day to be love of man to man.

It is not a new message. It has been preached before — among others, by the Christians who condemn Tolstoï as a fanatic and a dreamer; but Count Tolstoï is the first among moderns to show in a large way how the preaching may be carried into practice. The message may be, as some say it is, socialism or communism in disguise, but every thoughtful person will agree that it is a very harmless sort of communism, that it is, at any rate, better than anarchy, and that its influence upon mankind, for the present at least, cannot result in serious harm. The time may come when, as several pulpit orators have declared, the practice of the Golden Rule will subvert civilization, but the danger of such a social transformation is not pressing ; we may safely leave it to posterity with several other problems concerning which we are perplexing ourselves to-day.

In the book now before us, the latest of Count Tolstoï's published writings, we have still another polemical work. Taking that most dramatic and terrible manifestation of the war-like spirit, Napoleon's campaign in Russia, as an example, he undertakes to lay bare " The Physiology of War."

We do not need to read far in the volume before getting at his purpose. He vindicates once more the essential dignity of manhood. He would show that war is something more than a game on the part of sovereigns and diplomatists, that it lies deeper down in the very nature of things, that it is an expression of popular expansion, and that emperors, kings, commanders, generals, what not, are so many figure-heads, the toys of circumstance, passive instruments in the hands of destiny.

It will be seen at once that Count Tolstoï's philosophy of history takes a wide range and goes deep. It is the modern, the democratic spirit applied to the most terrible of human problems, war. It regards the common soldier as more than the general, and it sets forth with convincing eloquence the contrast between the ostensible leaders in a great struggle, the men who stand at the head and think they are directing the progress of events, and the real

actors in those events, the men who do the
work and bear the suffering — the common
soldiers.

In the course of this exposition, Count
Tolstoï does indeed reveal the very physiology
of war. No one knows better than he how a
war is conducted, what are the conditions of a
battle ; but the vital interest of this book is in
its portrayal of that mysterious force slowly
generated in the heart of Europe during the
revolutionary period, breaking out now and
then in random explosions, and at length
bursting all bounds, like a wave of fire bearing
Napoleon on its crest, rushing towards the
East, to Moscow, and to destruction — extin-
guished as it were in the frost and snow of
Russia.

With regard to Napoleon, the hero-worship-
per of the Carlylean stamp will find little in
this book to please him. The Man of Destiny
cuts here a most disreputable figure. His glo-
rious plumes have been stripped from him ere
this, but never yet has he come forth from the
pitiless hands of criticism so featherless, naked,
and contemptible a biped. " This," Count Tol-

stoï seems to say to us, "is your great man. I
show you great men." He will have no talk of
isolated genius guiding humanity to predetermined ends. Genius is to him not the guider,
but the guided, the exponent of fate, the bit
of steel that follows the invisible magnet of
destiny and indicates upon the dial of history
the course of what is and is to be. And then,
in the parable of the bee, Count Tolstoï sets
forth the conclusion of the whole matter, a conclusion old as the Book of Job, — "*Touching
the Eternal, we cannot find him out ; he is excellent in power.*"

If the Russian text of this book had been accessible, I should not have undertaken this version. But the Russian text is not at present to
be had ; it is doubtful if it has passed the ordeal
of censorship, and so, in default of a better, it is
hoped that the public will accept this attempt
with a kindly eye to its possible and probable
shortcomings. M. Michel Delines, whose French
interpretation I have followed, is an author of
repute, and I hope that, in keeping as closely
as possible in his footsteps, I have not strayed

far from the proper path.　If this version of "The Physiology of War" shall receive the approval given by Count Tolstoï to the writer's translation of "My Religion," I shall have reason to be more than content.

HUNTINGTON SMITH.

Dorchester, Mass., December 23, 1887.

NAPOLEON'S
RUSSIAN CAMPAIGN.

I.

PLAN OF THE CAMPAIGN OF 1812.

FRENCH authors, in the books which they have devoted to the history of the Russian campaign, are always trying to prove that Napoleon foresaw the danger involved in an extension of his line, that he sought by every means to give battle, and that his generals all advised him to halt at Smolensk. In other words, the historians in question advance all sorts of arguments to demonstrate that Napoleon and his staff understood beforehand the perils of the campaign.

Russian historians, on the contrary, are still more urgent in their attempts to persuade us that at the beginning of the campaign the plan by which Napoleon was to be enticed into the heart of Russia was already conceived. The plan is attributed to Pfühl, to Toll, to an unknown Frenchman, even to the Emperor Alexander himself. In support of their assertions they cite memoirs, suggestions, letters, in which allusions to such a plan of campaign are found.

But it is clear that all these so-called indications of foreknowledge have been seized upon by Russian and by French historians, simply because they are justified by what actually took place. If the war had taken a different course, these predictions would have been forgotten like many other conjectures that were not verified and yet were equally popular at the time.

Every event involves so many suppositions as to results that there will always be people who will have the right to say, "I told you this would happen," and we forget that among the predictions offered there were also many indicating just the contrary of what comes to pass.

To ascribe to Napoleon knowledge of the danger involved in an advance, and to credit the Russians with a plan for inveigling the enemy into the heart of the country, is to make

prophecies after the event. Historians cannot
attribute divination to Napoleon or strategical
projects to the Russians without forcing the
facts.

The truth is that throughout the whole campaign the Russians never dreamed of drawing
the French into the heart of their country; but
directed all their efforts to checking the advance of the enemy, from the moment that the
invasion was an accomplished fact.

Napoleon, on the other hand, not only did
not doubt the policy of advance, he treated
every onward movement as a triumph, and, in
contrast to his usual tactics, we find that in
this campaign he was not at all eager to give
battle.

As for us, from the beginning of the campaign we see our armies cut in two, and we are
occupied solely with the effort to bring them
into combined action. If we had desired to
simulate retreat, to draw the enemy on, there
would have been no advantage in reuniting our
dissevered troops. At length, Alexander I.
comes in person into the field, to inspire the
army by his presence to stubborn resistance,

and not to encourage a retreat. Then we form the great camp at Drissa, according to Pfühl's design, and any thought of retreat is out of the question. The tsar reproaches his generals for a single backward step. Alexander does not plan the burning of Smolensk; he does not desire that the enemy shall approach the walls of the city. When the combination of forces is at length effected, the tsar is angry at thinking that Smolensk has been taken and burned without an effort at defence.

Such are the views of the sovereign. As for the generals in command, they are as indignant as the troops at any suggestion of retreating before the enemy. .

Meanwhile, Napoleon, after cutting our armies asunder, marches on into the interior of the country, and allows several opportunities for giving battle to pass by unimproved. By August he is at Smolensk, intent upon a further advance into Russia, although this movement, as we see now, could only be fatal to his hopes.

The facts prove beyond doubt that Napoleon did not foresee the danger of an advance upon Moscow, and that Alexander I. and the Rus-

sian generals never dreamed of trying to draw
him into the heart of the country.

Napoleon was led on, not by any plan, — a
plan had never been thought of, — but by the
intrigues, quarrels, and ambition of men who
unconsciously played a part in this terrible war
and never foresaw that the result would be the
safety of Russia.

Everything goes on in the most unexpected
way. Our armies are divided at the outset of
the campaign. We endeavor to reunite them
with the evident object of giving battle and
checking the invasion, but our troops, while
seeking to effect a juncture, avoid battle with
the enemy, recognizing his strength ; our lines,
therefore, tend to form an acute angle, and the
French are drawn as far as Smolensk. The
acute angle is not solely due to the fact that the
enemy is moving between our two armies ;
another cause tends to diminish the angle and
favor our retreat. At the head of one of our
armies is Barclay de Tolly, a German, very unpopular with us. The commander of the other
army is Bagration, who has a personal hatred
against Barclay de Tolly and endeavors as far

as possible to delay the combination in order that he may not be subjected to Barclay's orders. Bagration succeeds in delaying the movement which is the chief object of all the Russian generals. He explains his action by saying that his troops are in danger and that it is better for him to draw off on the left and toward the south in order to harass the enemy on the flank and in the rear, and finally bring about the union of the armies in the Ukraine. But these excuses are only pretexts. The real cause of his policy of delay is a desire not to subject himself to the hated German, who is, moreover, of a rank inferior to his own.

The Emperor Alexander is with the army to inspire the troops by his presence, but he is surrounded by so many conflicting advisers, so many different plans are submitted to him, that he is unable to come to a decision. His hesitation paralyzes the energy of the army, and it finally beats a retreat.

The plan then is to entrench in the camp at Drissa, when suddenly Paulucci, who aspires to be commander-in-chief, gets such a hold upon the emperor that Pfühl's plan is abandoned.

The task of opposing the enemy is confided to Barclay, but, as he is not able to inspire much confidence, his power is limited.

Here, then, are the isolated armies, and a discordant command. Barclay is unpopular, and his unpopularity, together with the separation of the armies, produces the uncertainty which leads us to evade an encounter with the enemy.

If the union of the armies had been accomplished, and if Barclay had not been designated as commander-in-chief, a battle would have been inevitable. But circumstances served continually to increase the feeling against the Germans, and patriotism was more and more exalted.

Finally the tsar leaves the army, with the excuse that he is needed at Moscow and St. Petersburg to arouse the people and incite a national defence. In fact, the emperor's journey to Moscow triples the strength of the Russian troops.

Now, the truth is that the tsar withdraws from the army in order that he may not interfere with the power of the commander-in-chief.

He hopes that, in his absence, Barclay will take decisive measures. But the generals are more and more confused and helpless. Bennigsen, the grand-duke, and all his train of adjutants-general, remain in the army to spy out the intentions of the commander-in-chief and to favor energetic action. Barclay, under the eyes of these imperial censors, grows still more cautious, abstains from any decided operation, and carefully avoids giving battle.

Barclay's attitude leads the grand-duke to insinuate suspicions of treason and to advise a general attack. Lubomirski, Branitzki, Vlotzki, and other officers, make such an uproar that Barclay, to rid himself of them, sends the Polish adjutants-general to St. Petersburg with pretended messages of importance for the tsar, and enters upon open warfare with Bennigsen and the grand-duke.

At last, against the will of Bagration, the union of the two armies is effected, at Smolensk.

Bagration drives to Barclay's headquarters. The commander-in-chief emerges from the house and salutes his visitor as a superior in

rank. Overcome by this display of magnanimity, Bagration places himself under Barclay's
command, while remaining in spirit opposed to
the ideas of his chief. In the reports addressed
to Araktshïef at the express order of the tsar,
he said : —

"The will of the emperor be done, but I cannot stay
with the *ministre* (Barclay). . . . For the love of God, send
me where you will, give me only a single regiment to command, but do not leave me here, for I cannot stay. . . . The
quarters are full of Germans, and it is not possible for a
Russian to breathe here . . . the most idiotic things take
place. . . . When I believe that I am serving the tsar and
my country, I am really serving Barclay. . . . I confess that
this does not suit me."

The intrigues of Branitzki, of Wintzengerod,
and other superior officers embitters still further
the relations of the two chiefs, and united action is more and more impossible.

When the Russians are finally ready to attack the French at Smolensk, the commander-
in-chief sends a general to inspect the lines.
This general, hating Barclay, instead of obeying orders, goes to one of his friends, a corps
commander, remains with him all day, and
returns at night to Barclay, to disapprove of

a plan of battle which he has not even examined.

Amid these quarrels and intrigues, we are trying to meet the French, although ignorant of their whereabouts. The French encounter Neverovski's division, and approach the walls of Smolensk. It is impossible not to give battle at Smolensk. We must maintain our communications. The battle takes place, and thousands of men on both sides are killed.

Contrary to the wishes of the tsar and the people, our generals abandon Smolensk. The inhabitants of Smolensk, betrayed by their governor, set fire to the city, and, with this example to other Russian towns, they take refuge in Moscow, deploring their losses and sowing on every side the seeds of hate against the enemy.

Napoleon advances and we retreat, and the result is that we take exactly the measures necessary to conquer the French.

II.

THE TRUTH ABOUT THE BATTLE OF BORODINO.

FOR what reason and in what manner was the battle of Borodino fought? It had no meaning either for the Russians or the French. The immediate result of the battle was for the Russians what they most dreaded, a retreat to Moscow; and for the French what they feared more than anything else, the entire destruction of their army. Now, although this result was the only one possible, and might have been clearly foreseen, Napoleon offered battle, and Koutouzof accepted the challenge.

If he had been a commander governed by reasonable motives, Napoleon would have seen clearly that at twelve hundred miles from his own country he could not engage in a battle involving the possible loss of a fourth of his army without marching to certain destruction. In like manner Koutouzof might have seen clearly that a battle which exposed him to a loss of a fourth of his army would result at the same time in the loss of Moscow.

This is mathematically as evident as it would be in a game of draughts where, if I have one man less than my adversary, and by exchanging would certainly lose, I ought not to exchange.

When my adversary has sixteen men and I have only fourteen, I am only an eighth weaker than he; but when I shall have exchanged thirteen men, he will be three times stronger than I.

Up to the time of the battle of Borodino the Russian forces were to the French forces in the proportion of five to six; after the battle the proportion was only one to two. That is to say, before the battle the proportion was 100 : 120, and after the battle, 50 : 100. And yet Koutouzof, that intelligent and experienced general, accepted battle.

Napoleon, man of genius as he is called, fought this battle, which destroyed a fourth of his army and obliged him to continue his advance.

The objection may perhaps be made that Napoleon expected to end the campaign by the occupation of Moscow, as he had ended another campaign by the occupation of Vienna ; but we have sufficient evidence for thinking that such was not his idea. The historians most favorable to Napoleon assert that he wished to end his advance at Smolensk, because of the danger of extending his lines, and because he knew very well that the capture of Moscow would not end the campaign. He had seen at Smolensk how the Russians got their towns ready for him, and when he offered parley he met with no response.

Napoleon, in offering battle at Borodino, and Koutouzof, in accepting battle, acted each entirely contrary to the dictates of common-sense. But now come the historians, and, to justify accomplished facts, they have brought together an ingenious tissue of foresight and genius on the part of the commanders, whereas, in truth, these commanders were the most passive and involuntary instruments of all the involuntary instruments that ever served in the execution of great historical events.

The ancients have left us a number of historical poems, in which the interest is concentrated upon a few heroic figures, and we do not yet readily see that, in our more human times, this manner of regarding history is wholly without reason.

The second question is, How was the battle of Borodino and that of Shevardino, which preceded it, fought? The reply of the historians is not less positive, as every one knows. They all agree in telling us that:—

" *The Russian army, in its so-called retreat from Smolensk, sought the most favorable position for a general battle, and found it at Borodino.*

" *The Russians had beforehand fortified this position on the left of the road, almost in a right angle from Borodino to Oustitsa, the point, in fact, where the battle took place.*

" *To keep watch of the enemy, they established in front a fortified redoubt upon the hills of Shevardino. On the 5th of September, Napoleon attacked the redoubt, and took it by assault; September 7, he attacked the entire Russian army, which was then in position on the fields of Borodino.*"

Such is the story of all the historians, and it is absolutely false, as those who examine the matter may readily see.

The Russians did not look for the most favorable position. On the contrary, they passed, during their retreat, several positions far superior to that of Borodino. They did not pause at any of these positions, for various reasons. Koutouzof would accept only a place that was of his own choosing; the necessity of a general battle had not yet made itself clearly felt; finally, Miloradovitch had not yet arrived with reënforcements; — and there were other reasons, that cannot be enumerated here. From these considerations it appears that the first positions of the Russian army were stronger than the position at Borodino, and that this position was not only unfavorable in itself, but that, by sticking a pin anywhere at hap-hazard into the map of Russia, a better place might have been found.

Moreover, the Russians had not fortified the position on the left of Borodino at a right angle with the road; up to September 6, 1812, they never imagined that the battle would occur at this point. To prove this, I maintain, in the first place, that on September 6 there was no fortification, for the work of entrenching began on that day, and was not ended till September 7; and, in the second place, I will describe the position of the Shevardino redoubt — for to put this redoubt in front of the position where the battle was fought is simply nonsensical. Why was this redoubt more strongly fortified than all the other defensive points? Why did the Russian army exhaust itself and sacrifice six thousand men in futile efforts to hold this redoubt as late as the night of September 5? A Cossack patrol amply sufficed to keep watch of the enemy.

To demonstrate that the battle was not fought at a point anticipated by the Russian army, and that the redoubt at Shevardino was not an advance post of this position, I have a third proof, still more conclusive than the others. Up to September 6, Barclay de Tolly and Bagration believed that the Shevardino redoubt was on the left flank of their position, and Koutouzof himself, while the impressions of the combat were still fresh in his mind, wrote a report in which he spoke of the Shevardino redoubt as on the left flank.

It is evident that later on, when there was time for reflection, they got up a story to smooth over the mistakes of the commander-in-chief, who would be nothing less than infallible. They said that the Shevardino redoubt was an advance post, whereas in reality it was only a fortification on the left flank, and they maintained that the battle of Borodino had occurred at a position which they had chosen and fortified beforehand. The truth is that the battle took place where it was least expected to occur and at a point that was not fortified at all.

The real state of things was as follows : —

A position was chosen upon the Kolotsha river, which crosses the highway, not at a right angle, but at an acute angle, and consequently the left flank rested on Shevardino, the right flank was near the village of Novoë, while the centre was at Borodino, at the confluence of the two rivers Kolotsha and Voïna. This position, covered by the Kolotsha river, was held by an army which sought to check the enemy in his march upon Moscow by the road from

Smolensk. Whoever will look over the field of Borodino, putting out of his mind the stories that have been told about the battle, will certainly come to this conclusion.

Napoleon, on September 5, was moving towards Valouëvo; he had not discovered, the historians gravely tell us, a position of the Russians from Oustitsa to Borodino — for the very good reason that they were not there. Neither did he see the advance post of the Russian army, but, pursuing the Russian rearguard, he hurled himself upon the Shevardino redoubt on the left flank of the Russians and took them by surprise by passing with his troops across the Kolotsha. The Russians, not having succeeded in bringing about a general engagement, drew back their left wing, abandoning the position which they had intended to occupy, and taking another, of which they had not thought, and which was wholly without fortifications.

When Napoleon had crossed from the left bank of the Kolotsha, he transposed the centre of hostilities from right to left with reference to the Russian army, and brought it into the tract of country between Oustitsa, Semenovskoë, and Borodino. This place, as we have said, had no advantage over any other for the Russians, but here it was that the battle of September 7 was fought.

The subjoined rough sketch shows the plan of the supposed battle, and that of the battle which actually took place.

If on the night of September 5 Napoleon had not moved in the direction of the Kolotsha, and, instead of giving the order to attack the redoubt immediately, had reserved his attack until the next morning, no one would have doubted that Shevardino was on the left flank of the Russian position, and the battle would have taken place as the Russians expected. In that case, the Russians would have defended the redoubt still more stubbornly in order to protect their left flank ; they would have attacked Napoleon in the centre or on the right ; and on September 5 the battle would have occurred in the position they had chosen and fortified. But as the attack upon the left flank of the Russian army took place at night, following the retreat of the rear-guard, and immediately after the battle of

Gridnevo, and as the Russians would not or
could not begin a general engagement on September 5, — the first and the most important
action in the battle of Borodino was lost on the
5th of September, and this led inevitably to
the loss of the battle fought on September 7.

When the French had carried the Shevardino
redoubt, the Russians were without protection
on the left flank, and were obliged to withdraw
their left wing and fortify themselves as chance
and urgency demanded.

Thus on September 7 the Russian troops
were not only provided with weak and incom-
plete entrenchments, but the disadvantages of
their position were increased by the refusal
of their commanders to recognize the facts.
They refused to admit that their position on
the left flank was lost, and that the battle-
ground had been transferred from right to
left. So the Russian army, refusing to mod-
ify its extended position reaching from the
village of Novoë to Oustitsa, was obliged during the engagement to transfer troops from
right to left. Consequently, the Russians confronted the French army, which was directed

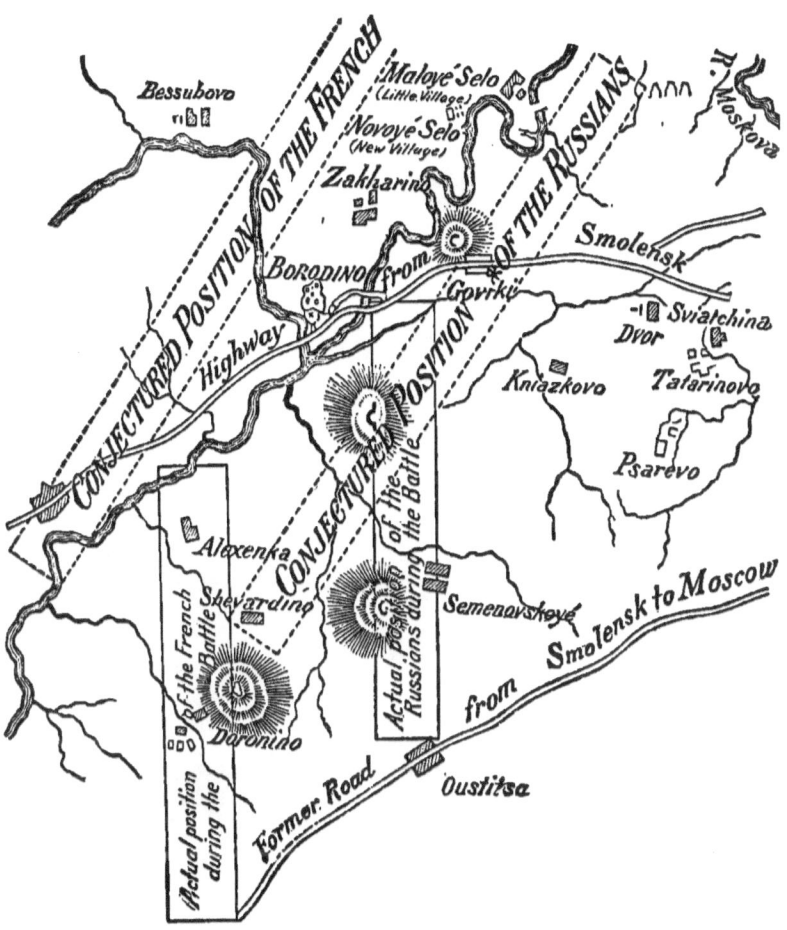

upon their left flank, with a force twice inferior to that of the enemy.

Poniatovski's movements against Oustitsa
and Ouvarovo, on the right flank of the French,
were independent incidents in the progress
of the battle.

Thus the battle of Borodino did not take
place in conformity with the assertions of historians, who wish to conceal the mistakes of
our chiefs, and who in this way detract from
the glory which belongs to the Russian army
and the Russian people. The battle of Borodino did not occur at a place chosen and
fortified beforehand, neither were the Russian forces nearly equal to those of the
French. The fact is that by the loss of the
Shevardino redoubt the Russians were brought
face to face in an unfortified position with an
enemy outnumbering them two to one. Under
these conditions it was impossible for them
to hold their own for ten consecutive hours,.
impossible even to save the army from complete defeat after a three-hours engagement.

III.

NAPOLEON'S PREPARATIONS FOR THE BATTLE OF BORODINO.

ACCORDING to the historians, Napoleon passed the entire day of September 6 on horseback, inspecting the battle-field, examining the plans offered by his marshals, and dictating orders to his staff.

The Russian lines had been modified, and the capture of the Shevardino redoubt had forced a retreat of the left flank. This position was not fortified, or protected by the river, and before it extended a naked, level plain.

It is evident to any one, whether military or not, that this weak spot is where the French ought to make their attack. To reach this conclusion there was no need of so many combinations and preparations on the part of the emperor and his marshals. That high and extraordinary capacity which

we call genius, and which is so commonly
attributed to Napoleon, was on this occasion
entirely superfluous. And yet the historians
who have described these events, the men
who surrounded Napoleon, and Napoleon himself, thought differently.

Napoleon, they tell us, rode over the ground
which he had chosen for a battle, examined
the country, profoundly absorbed in his re-
flections, moving his head in sign of approval
or disapproval, as if in answer to his own
thoughts, and without deigning to reveal to
the generals about him the profound ideas
that influenced his decisions. To them he
gave only definite results in the form of
orders. Davoust, otherwise called the Duke
of Eckmühl, proposed to turn the right flank
of the Russians; Napoleon rejected this proposition without saying why he did so. To
the suggestion of General Campan, who was
to attack Bagration's outworks, and who offered to lead his division through the woods,
Napoleon gave his consent, although Ney,
the so-called Duke of Elchingen, observed
that the march through the woods would be

dangerous, and would throw the division into disorder.

Napoleon, after examining the country in front of the Shevardino redoubt, remained for some time in meditation ; then he ordered the placing of two batteries, for the bombardment of the Russian fortifications on the following day, and he selected positions for the field-artillery.

After giving his orders, he retired to his tent, and drew up in writing the plan of battle.

Here is the plan of which French historians speak with transports of praise, and which the historians of other nations treat with respect :

"ORDER OF BATTLE.

" *At the camp, two leagues in the rear of Mozhaïsk.*
" *September* 6, 1812.

" At daybreak the two new batteries constructed during the night on the plateau by the Prince of Eckmühl will open fire upon the two batteries of the enemy opposite.

" At the same moment, General Pernety, commanding the First Corps of Artillery, with thirty cannon from Campan's Division, and all the howitzers of Dessaix' and Friant's Divisions placed in advance, will begin shelling the enemy's battery, which, by this means, will have against it : —

" 24 pieces of guard,
" 30 from Campan's Division, and
" 8 from Friant's and Dessaix' Divisions.

" Total : 62 cannon.

" General Fouché, commanding the Third Corps of Artillery, will place himself with all the howitzers of the Third and Eighth Corps, which are sixteen in number, around the battery attacking the left redoubt, giving this battery a force of 40 pieces.

" General Sorbier will stand ready, at the word of command, with all the howitzers of the guard, to repair to one or the other redoubt.

" During the cannonade, Prince Poniatovski will move from the village towards the woods, and turn the position of the enemy.

" General Campan will move along the edge of the woods, to carry the first redoubt.

" The battle thus begun, orders will be given according to the disposition of the enemy.

" The cannonade on the left will begin at the moment when that on the right is heard. A heavy infantry fire will be begun by Morand's Division, and by the Divisions of the Viceroy, as soon as they see that the attack on the right has commenced.

" The Viceroy will take possession of the village,[1] and debouch by the three bridges to the heights, while Generals Morand and Gérard will deploy under the orders of the Viceroy to seize the enemy's redoubt and form the line of battle.

" All this must be done with order and method, taking care always to exercise the greatest caution."

This order, not very clear in its style, will appear very confusing to any one so far de-

[1] Borodino.

ficient in religious veneration for the genius of Napoleon as to dare to analyze its meaning. It contains four commands, of which not one was executed, because it was impossible to carry them out.

The first command was as follows: —

"The batteries established at the points chosen by Napoleon, with the cannon of Pernety and Fouché, will place themselves in line, one hundred and two pieces in all, and, opening fire, will devastate the Russian outworks and redoubts."

This command could not be followed, because from the place chosen by Napoleon the shots would not have reached the Russian entrenchments, and these one hundred and two cannon would have thundered in vain until the nearest commander had ordered them to the front, contrary to Napoleon's decree.

Here is the second command: —

"Poniatovski will move from the village towards the woods, and turn the left wing of the Russians."

This command could not be executed, because Poniatovski, on moving towards the woods, found Toutchkof barring the way, and he could not turn the position of the Russians.

The third command is that

"*General Campan will move along the edge of the woods and carry the first redoubt.*"

General Campan's Division did not take the first redoubt, because it was repulsed; on emerging from the woods, it was obliged to close up under the Russian fire, something that Napoleon had not foreseen.

The fourth command is this : —

"*The Viceroy will take possession of the village* [Borodino], *and will debouch by its three bridges upon the heights, while Generals Morand and Gérard* [who are not told either where or when they ought to go] *will deploy under the orders of the Viceroy to seize the enemy's redoubt and form the line of battle.*"

As far as it is possible to understand this (relying more upon the efforts of the Viceroy to carry out the orders he received than upon the vague phraseology in which they were given), it seems that he was told to move from Borodino upon the redoubt at the left, and that Morand's and Gérard's Divisions were at the same time to advance the front.

This command, like all the rest, was not carried out. because it was wholly impracticable.

When he had got beyond Borodino, the Viceroy was forced back upon the Kolotsha, and found it impossible to advance. Morand's and Gérard's Divisions did not take any redoubts, because they were repulsed. The redoubt was carried by the cavalry at the close of the battle, by a possibility that Napoleon had not foreseen. We see, therefore, that not one of the commands in this order was performed.

The order further asserted that during the battle instructions would be given in accordance with the movements of the enemy. From this we might infer that Napoleon, during the battle, made all the suggestions that were necessary. He did nothing of the sort. The facts do not fail to show that he was so far away from the field of action that the progress of the battle was not even known to him.

IV.

HOW FAR NAPOLEON'S WILL INFLUENCED THE BATTLE OF BORODINO.

SEVERAL historians assure us that the victory of the French at Borodino was modified by the fact that Napoleon was suffering from the effects of a cold in the head. If it had not been for this cold, his arrangements before and during the battle would have displayed still more genius, Russia would have been conquered, and *the face of the world would have been changed.*

Historians who believe that Russia was formed at the will of one man, Peter the Great; who believe that France changed from a republic to an empire and sent armies to Russia at the will of one man, Napoleon, naturally think that Russia retained some vestige of power after the battle of Borodino because Napoleon had a cold in his head on September 7; — and they are logically consistent in thinking so.

Plainly, if it depended on the will of Napoleon to give or not to give battle at Borodino, to make or not to make such and such dispositions of his forces, it is evident that the cold in his head, which influenced the manifestation of his will, must have been of great service to the Russian cause, and that the valet who, on September 5, 1812, forgot to provide Napoleon with waterproof boots was the real savior of Russia. When we have once started on this line of reasoning, the conclusion is inevitable; as much so as that reached by the ironical Voltaire when he demonstrated that the Massacre of Saint Bartholomew was due to the fact that Charles IX. suffered from indigestion.

But to those who do not believe that Russia was formed at the will of Peter the Great, that the French empire arose at the bidding of a single man, or that the campaign in Russia was undertaken at the sole behest of Napoleon, such reasoning will appear to be not only unreasonable and false, but contrary to the nature of human activity. To them the response to the question, What is the cause of historical events? is something very different. They believe that the progress of events is inevitable ; that it is a result of the combined volition of all who participate in the events, and that the influence of Napoleons upon the progress of affairs is superficial and fictitious.

It is paradoxical to assert that the Massacre of Saint Bartholomew was the work of Charles IX. because he gave the order to kill, and believed that the killing was done at his command. Not less paradoxical is it to affirm that the battle of Borodino, which cost the lives of eighty thousand men, was the work of Napoleon because he planned the engagement, and gave the order to begin the attack. A sentiment of human dignity, which tells me that each of us, if he be not more of a man than Napoleon the Great, is at least not less than he, directs me to a solution of the problem justified by a multitude of facts.

At the battle of Borodino, Napoleon did not attack anybody or kill anybody. That duty was performed by his soldiers. He did not do any killing himself. The soldiers of the French army, in going to the battle of Borodino to kill Russian soldiers, were obeying,

not Napoleon's orders, but their own impulses.
The whole army of French, Italians, Germans,
Poles, famished and in rags, worn out by the
campaign, felt, at sight of the Russian army
barring the road to Moscow, that the wine was
uncorked, and they had only to rush in and
drink. If at this moment Napoleon had for-
bidden them to fight the Russians, they would
have killed him and given battle ; for to them a
battle was necessary. When they heard the
proclamations of Napoleon which, in exchange
for wounds and death, offered them as a conso-
lation the homage of posterity, and proclaimed
as heroes those who should fight through the
Muscovite campaign, they cried, "Vive l'Empereur ! " — as they cried "Vive l'Empereur ! "
at sight of the child holding the terrestrial
globe at the end of a bilboquet stick ; and they
would have responded with the same *vivat* to
any nonsense proffered to them. There was
nothing better for them to do than to cry
"Vive l'Empereur ! " and fight in order to reach
Moscow, food, repose, and victory. It was not
at Napoleon's order that they undertook to kill
their fellow-men.

The progress of the battle was not directed by Napoleon, for no part of his plan was carried out ; and during the engagement he did not know what was going on before his eyes.

Hence the manner in which these men undertook to kill one another was independent of Napoleon and not influenced by the action of his will, because it was determined by the will of the thousands of men who took part in the combat. *But it seemed to Napoleon as if his will was the main-spring of action.*

Thus we see that the question, " Did or did not Napoleon have a cold in his head ? " is of no more importance to the historian than a cold in the head of the last stragglers from the ranks.

The fact that Napoleon was afflicted with a cold in the head on September 7 is still more insignificant because it is easy to prove the falsity of the assertions made by writers that by reason of this cold in the head Napoleon's dispositions and orders concerning the battle were less adroit than those he was accustomed to make.

The plan, which we have already given, is

not at all inferior — it is even superior — to plans that in his preceding campaigns led him to victory. The fictitious combinations prepared for this battle were not in the least inferior to those of previous battles; they were, in fact, of absolutely equivalent value. But the dispositions and the combinations seem less fortunate, because the battle of Borodino was the first battle that Napoleon did not win. The best plan and the most sagacious combinations in the world seem very poor when they do not end in victory, and the veriest tyro in military matters does not hesitate to criticise them. On the other hand, the feeblest plans and combinations appear to be excellent when they are crowned with success, and learned men devote entire volumes to the demonstration of their superiority.

The plan proposed by Weirother for the battle of Austerlitz was a model of its kind, but it was condemned because its very perfection involved a superabundance of details.

Napoleon at the battle of Borodino played his sovereign part as well as in other battles — even better. He did nothing that could stand in the way of success; he accepted the most reasonable advice; he did not confuse his orders, he did not contradict himself, he was exempt from weakness, he did not abandon the field of battle, — with all his tact and his great experience in war, he assumed with calmness and dignity the part of a fictitious commander.

V.

THE RETREAT TO FILY.

THE united forces of twenty European nations have entered Russia. The Russian army
and the people recoil before the enemy as far
as Smolensk, and from Smolensk to Borodino.
The French army, with continually increasing
velocity, advances upon Moscow, its chosen destination.

As it approaches this point, its progress becomes more rapid, just as the velocity of a
falling body increases as it draws near the
earth. The French army has behind it thousands of miles of devastated country ; before it,
only a few miles off, the goal of all its efforts.
Every soldier in Napoleon's army knows that he
is nearing the end, and the army moves forward
propelled by the force of its own momentum.

In the Russian army, a spirit of fury arises
against the enemy, and this spirit becomes more
and more inflamed by retreat.

At Borodino the two armies meet.

Neither one nor the other is dispersed, but immediately after the collision the Russian army recoils, as surely as a cannon-ball recoils when struck by another in full flight. At the same time the invading body moves, no less surely, a certain distance forward, although the impelling force has been diminished by the shock.

The Russians retire to a point about fifty miles from Moscow, while the French enter the city and come to a standstill.

During the five weeks that follow, no battle is fought. The French give no signs of life.

Like an animal mortally wounded, licking the blood that issues from its wounds, the French remain for five weeks at Moscow doing nothing. Then suddenly, with no apparent reason, they fly backward, take the road to Kalouga, and, although the field of Malo-Yaro-slavetz is theirs, they retreat still more rapidly to Smolensk, without fighting any important battle, and from Smolensk retire to Vilna, from Vilna to the Beresina, and so on, going always further away.

On the night of September 7, Koutouzof and

the Russian army believe that they have won the battle. Koutouzof even makes a report to that effect to the Tsar Alexander I.

Koutouzof had given an order to prepare for another battle to finish with the enemy, not at all with the intention of giving an erroneous impression, but because he knew that the enemy had been beaten. The fact was that both sides were beaten in this battle.

But when, that night and all the next day, news comes in of the terrible losses sustained by the army, which is reduced to one-half of its former strength, it becomes clear that another battle is physically impossible.

How can they undertake another battle without informing themselves of their condition, with the wounded uncared for, the dead uncounted, their instruments of warfare destroyed, their dead generals not replaced, and their men unrefreshed by food and sleep?

Meanwhile, the French army, after the battle, with a centrifugal force seemingly augmented inversely by the square of the distance, has heaped itself upon the Russian ranks.

Koutouzof wanted to renew the attack on the

morrow, and his army was with him in this
desire.   But it is not enough to desire a thing
to do it.   Desire alone will not justify an attack ;
it must also be possible, and in this case possibility was lacking.

There was no way to prevent first one days
march in retreat, then a second, then a third,
and when, on September 13, the army was
before Moscow, although the troops had re-
gained their courage, circumstances obliged
them to retire behind the city.   They made
this retrograde movement and abandoned Moscow to the enemy.

To those who imagine that generals plan their
campaign and battles as we, seated tranquilly
in our libraries with a map spread before us,
make up combinations and ask ourselves what
measures ought to be taken in such and such a
war, to such persons I propound this question :
Why did not Koutouzof, in beating a retreat, find
some position before reaching Fily ? — why did
he not follow the road to Kalouga, leaving
Moscow to take care of itself ?   Other similar
questions suggest themselves.

Now, the fact is that the persons of whom we

have been speaking take no account of the inevitable conditions in which a commander-in-chief must act. His situation is not at all what we imagine it to be when we picture him comfortably seated in his study, planning, with the aid of a map, a campaign against a given number of the enemy, moving in a determined direction and during a definite period of time.

When action begins, the general-in-chief is never surrounded by conditions such as we have at command when we examine the event seated tranquilly at our library tables. The commander-in-chief is always at the centre of a series of events so complex and so hurried that it is not possible for a single instant to comprehend the importance of what is going on. The result is invisible, details are unfolded from hour to hour, and during all the changes of their continuous progress the commander-in-chief is at the centre of a complicated game of perplexities, responsibilities, projects and counsels, subject to all manner of danger and deceit, and obliged to reply to innumerable and contradictory questions.

Military critics assert in the most serious

manner that Koutouzof might have led his troops
in the direction of Kalouga before retreating to
Fily, and they even say that such a course was
suggested to him.   They forget that at a decisive moment a commander-in-chief has not only
one proposal but a dozen proposals to examine.
All plans based upon strategy and tactics are
mutually contradictory.   Theoretically, it is the
office of the commander-in-chief to select some
one of the plans that are suggested, but he has
not the leisure to compare and decide between
them.   Events will not wait for him.

Suppose that on September 10 the proposal
is made to Koutouzof to take the route to
Kalouga, but that at the same moment an adjutant from Miloradovitch comes up at a gallop
and asks whether they shall begin an attack
upon the French or retreat.   This question
must be answered at once, and the suggestion
turns Koutouzof's attention from the plans of
retreating by Kalouga.

But following the adjutant comes the commissary to ask whither the stores are to be
transported ;   then the chief of ambulance
wishes to know what is to be done with the

wounded; and finally arrives a courier from St.
Petersburg bearing a message from the tsar
declaring the abandonment of Moscow to be
impossible.

Meanwhile, a rival of the commander-in-chief
— and there is always at least one ready to sap
his authority — presents a new plan, directly
opposed to that favoring retreat by the road to
Kalouga. The commander-in-chief is thoroughly exhausted and must at any cost have
rest and sleep. This consideration does not
prevent the general who has not been decorated
from making a complaint; the people of the
country implore protection; an officer who has
been sent out to reconnoitre returns with the
report directly contrary to that of the officer
who preceded him, a spy (poor captive) has
still another version, the general who has made
the reconnaissance a third, — all describe differently the position of the enemy.

Those who do not take into account the inevitable conditions controlling the actions of
the commander-in-chief show us, for example,
the situation of the army at Fily, and start with
the idea that the general commanding had till

September 13 to debate the question whether or not to abandon the defence of Moscow, whereas with the Russian army within five versts of Moscow this question could not even arise.

At what point, then, was this question solved?

It was solved at Drissa, at Smolensk, still more plainly on September 5 at Shevardino, at Borodino on the 7th, and every day, every hour, and every minute of the retreat from Borodino to Fily.

VI.

MOSCOW ABANDONED BY ITS INHABITANTS.

THE abandonment of Moscow and the destruction of that city by fire were as inevitable as was the retreat of the army to the rear of Moscow, after the battle of Borodino, without any other conflict with the enemy.

All Russia could have predicted the course of events, not by the aid of logical reasoning, but by the light of patriotic sentiment, which burns in the heart of every Russian, and inspired all who took part in this historical drama.

What occurred at Moscow had occurred spontaneously after Smolensk in every town and village of the invaded territory, and this without the need of Count Rostoptchin's proclamations. The people waited calmly for the enemy. They were not agitated, they did not revolt, they did not tear anybody in pieces; they simply waited calmly for what was to happen, knowing that at the critical moment their course of action would be plain. As the enemy approached, the wealthier portion of the population fled, leaving their property; and the poor remained to burn and destroy what was left behind.

A consciousness that things cannot be different from what they really are has always been a trait of Russian character, and it still exists. A consciousness — more, a presentiment — that Moscow would be taken by the enemy was manifest in Muscovite society in 1812.

Those who forsook the ancient capital of Russia from the month of July to the beginning of August proved that they saw what was to follow.

Those who went away, carrying what they could with them and leaving their houses and a great part of their goods, were acting under the influence of that "latent" patriotism which does not manifest itself in phrases, or in the sacrifice of children for the safety of the country, or by any other similar and unnatural actions, but which is generated imperceptibly, simply, organically, and for that reason leads to the most significant results.

On every side the cry went up, " It is cow-
ardly to fly from danger ; only cowards will
abandon Moscow ! ''

Rostoptchin declared in his proclamations
that the abandonment of Moscow would be a
disgrace.

Those who went away were ashamed to hear
themselves spoken of as cowards ; they were
ashamed to go, and yet they went, feeling that
at the time there was nothing else to be done.

Why did they take to flight ? We cannot
believe that they were frightened by Rostoptchin's stories of atrocities committed by
Napoleon in the towns conquered by him.
The people who gave the signal for flight were
rich and cultivated. They knew that Vienna
and Berlin had remained intact during the
French occupation, and that the inhabitants of
those cities passed the time gayly with the
adorable Frenchmen, whom, at the period in
question, Russians, and especially Russian
ladies, greatly loved.

Moscow was abandoned because the Russians did not ask themselves whether they
would be comfortable or not under French

domination. They had no doubts whatever
about the matter. The greatest of all evils
was to remain under an enemy's rule.

Before Borodino they went away, and after
that battle they went still more rapidly, deaf
to the appeals of Rostoptchin, who begged
them to remain and defend the city; deaf to
his plea that they should go out to fight the
French, led by the shrine of the Holy Mother
of Yver; caring nothing for the balloons which
were to destroy Napoleon, or for any of the
nonsense with which Rostoptchin's proclamations were filled.

Those who took to flight knew that the army
would do its duty, and that, if it were not
victorious, they, with their daughters and their
valets, would not be able to fight Napoleon;
and so there was nothing for them to do but to
depart, in spite of their regrets at the loss of
their property.

They went away without thinking what a
grand spectacle it would be, this great and rich
capital abandoned by its inhabitants and delivered over to the flames, for a great city built of
wood, and deserted, is fatally certain to be

burned. They went away, each by himself,
and yet to them is due the great event which
will always be the greatest glory of the Russian
people.

That great Russian lady who in the month
of June fled from Moscow to Saratof, with her
troop of *négrillons* and comedians, feeling
vaguely that she would not serve Bonaparte,
and fearing that she would be arrested on the
road by order of Rostoptchin, accomplished
simply and in all sincerity the work which was
the salvation of Russia.

As for Count Rostoptchin, now he cried
shame upon all who deserted Moscow, and
then himself ordered the evacuation of the
government offices ; now he gave useless arms
to a mob of drunkards ; now he displayed the
sacred images in the streets, and then forbade
the Archbishop Augustin to take away the
holy relics; now he seized all private con-
veyances ; now he brought on one hundred
and thirty-six carts the balloon prepared by
Lepic ; now he made known his intention
to burn Moscow ; now he declared that he
set fire to his residence with his own hands

and at the same time sent a proclamation to
the French solemnly reproaching Napoleon for
having destroyed the Foundling Asylum ; now
he took credit for the burning of Moscow,
and then denied it ; now he commanded that
all spies should be seized and brought to him ;
now he left Madame Oberchalemet, the head
of the French society of the town, in peace,
and then gave orders for the expulsion of the
aged and respectable director of posts, Klout-
sharef ; now he convoked the people at the
Three Hills to fight the French, and then,
to rid himself of these people, he delivered to
them the unhappy Veretshagin for slaughter,
and escaped himself by one of the rear gates ;
now he declared that he should not survive
the disasters of Moscow ; now he wrote in
albums, to celebrate his conduct, French verses
like these : —

> " Je suis né tartare,
>   Je voulais être romain ;
> Les français m'appeleront barbare,
>   Les russes Georges Dandin."

This man had no comprehension whatever
of what was going on ; he wished only to do

something, to astonish somebody, to perform some act of patriotic heroism, and like a child, playing with that great and fatal event, the abandonment and burning of Moscow, he sought with his feeble hand now to force along, now to restrain, the vast wave of popular action which bore him onward.

VII.

THE BURNING OF MOSCOW.

THE burning of Moscow is by the French attributed to the ferocious patriotism of Rostoptchin ; by the Russians, to the savagery of the French. But the fact is, the burning of Moscow cannot be attributed to any one person or any number of persons who could be named.

Moscow burned because the city was in a condition when a city of wood must necessarily burn, even if we do not take into account the one hundred and thirty fire-engines, which were of little service or of no service at all. Moscow, in the absence of its inhabitants, was doomed to the flames ; the conflagration was inevitable, just as a heap of shavings upon which sparks are dropped must sooner or later take fire.

A wooden city which had its fires every day in spite of the police who watched, and the

proprietors who looked after their houses,
could not escape destruction when the inhabi-
tants-were replaced by troops of soldiers, who
smoked their pipes, made piles of senators'./
chairs for firewood in the senate assembling-
place, and there, twice a day, cooked their meals.

Even in times of peace, when troops take up
their quarters in villages, the number of fires
is immediately multiplied. How much greater
must the chances of conflagration be in a deserted city built of wood and occupied by a
foreign army !

The ferocious patriotism of Rostoptchin and
the savagery of the French had nothing to do
with the event. The burning of Moscow was
due to the soldiers' pipes, to the fires used in
cooking food, to the piles of wood, and to the
negligence of hostile troops, when the inhabitants were replaced by foreigners.

Even if there were incendiaries, which is
very doubtful, since no one would have cared
uselessly to have risked his life, they could not
be considered as the cause of the conflagration,
which would have taken place without them.

It is in vain for the French to condemn the

ferocious patriotism of Rostoptchin, or for the Russians to blame the malefactor Bonaparte, for placing the heroic torch in the hands of the people. We are forced to acknowledge that such causes had no real existence. Moscow was burned as any town would be burned, when the houses are abandoned by their legitimate occupants, and when strangers enter and take possession of the cuisine.

We may truthfully say that Moscow was burned by its inhabitants; not, however, by those who remained, but by those who went away.

Moscow, when occupied by the enemy, did not remain intact like Berlin, Vienna, and other capitals, because the inhabitants did not sally forth to greet the French with bread and salt and the keys of the city, — they preferred to abandon their houses to the enemy.

VIII.

THE FLANK MOVEMENT.

AFTER the battle of Borodino and the occupation and burning of Moscow, the most important episode of this campaign, as all the world agrees, is the movement of the Russian army when it forsook the route to Riazan, and moved by way of Kalouga toward the camp of Taroutino — in a word, the flank movement beyond Krasnaïa Pakhra.

Historians ascribe the glory of this movement to different persons, and do not agree upon any one name as the recipient of honor. Foreign historians, even the French, in speaking of this flank movement, pay homage to the genius of the chiefs of the Russian army.

But why do chroniclers of battles, and, in their turn, the historians, believe that this flank movement was the ingenious invention of a single person, who thus saved Russia and overthrew Napoleon ? That is something which I am unable to explain.

To begin with, it is not easy to understand why this movement indicates the quality of genius in him who devised it. To see that the best position for an unoccupied army is the place nearest a base of supply is something that does not require a great intellectual effort. A boy of thirteen would have been able to decide that in 1812 the best position for the Russian army after the retreat from Moscow would be on the road to Kalouga.

It is still more difficult to understand why historians assign the salvation of the Russians and the destruction of the French to the execution of this manœuvre ; for, if the movement had been carried out under other conditions, it would have been disastrous to the Russians and beneficial to the French. The situation of the Russian army was improved after this movement, but that is no reason for asserting that the movement was the ameliorating cause.

The movement in question was not only of no advantage to the Russians ; under other conditions it would have been fatal.

What would have happened if Moscow had not been burned? if Napoleon had taken the offensive instead of remaining inactive?

What if the Russian army had followed the advice of Bennigsen and Barclay, and had given battle at Krasnaïa Pakhra?

What would have been the result if the French had attacked the Russians when the latter were on the march beyond Pakhra?

What turn would events have taken if Napoleon, after approaching Taroutino, had attacked the Russians with even a tenth part of the energy displayed at Smolensk?

What would have happened if the French had directed their course toward St. Petersburg?

In every case, the flank movement, instead of being the salvation of Russia, would have been a source of disaster.

Still more incomprehensible is the inability of historians to see how impossible it is to attribute the idea of a flank movement to any particular person. No one could plan it beforehand. This manœuvre, like the retreat to Fily, never presented itself to anybody in its

totality, but was developed little by little, moment by moment, one event after another. It
was the result of divergent incidents, and it
appeared clearly as a definite movement only
when it had been consummated and was an
accomplished fact.

In the council of war held by the Russian
generals at Fily, the favorite opinion was for
direct retreat by the most obvious route, that
of Nishnei-Novgorod. The majority expressed
adherence to this plan. But Lanski, who was
in charge of the commissary department, informed the commander-in-chief that the army
stores were concentrated principally in the
provinces of Toula and Kalouga, and that if
the army retreated upon Nishnei-Novgorod, the
great river Oka would be between them and
their stores, and, with the advent of winter, cut
them off from their supplies.

This was the first indication of the necessity obliging the army to renounce the plan
of a direct retreat, which at first had seemed
so obvious.

The army moved southward, on the road
to Riazan, to be nearer its base of supply.

Then, the inactivity of the French who seemed to have lost sight of the Russian army, the necessity for protecting the arsenal at Toula, added to the advantage of proximity to supplies, induced the Russian army to move still further south on the road to Toula.

When at length Pakhra had been passed, and the army was moving on the way to Toula, the chiefs contemplated a halt at Podolsk, not thinking at all of taking up a position at Taroutino. Various circumstances — among others, the approach of the French army, plans for giving battle, and the abundance of stores collected at Kalouga — obliged the Russian army to continue its southerly course, and, instead of moving further on the route to Toula, to take the route to Kalouga and approach Taroutino.

We can no more tell who decided upon Taroutino as an objective point than we can tell when Moscow was abandoned.

When the troops, after going through a great many unforeseen experiences, got to Taroutino, certain persons began to think that matters had gone on thus far in accordance with their plans, and to believe that the course of events had for a long time been known to them.

The celebrated flank movement was very simple. The Russian army, moving back in a line directly opposite to that followed by the invaders, turned aside when the enemy no longer pursued, and naturally took the direction in which lay an abundance of supplies.

If the Russian army had been without a commanding general, it would nevertheless have made the return movement about Moscow, and continued in a direction where there were more provisions and where the country was better suited to its needs.

The change of route which led towards Riazan, Toula, and Kalouga, instead of toward Nishnei, was so natural that the foragers of the Russian army went readily in that direction, and it was the route, moreover, upon which Koutouzof had been ordered from St. Petersburg to conduct his troops.

On arriving at Taroutino, Koutouzof was blamed for having led his army in the direction of Riazan, and he was informed of his position in regard to Kalouga, while at the same time he received a letter from the tsar containing unmerited reproaches.

The Russian army is like a ball rolling in the direction of the impelling force of the campaign, and, after the battle of Borodino, as that force diminishes in power, tending toward a natural position.

The merit of Koutouzof does not lie in flights of strategical genius, but is due to the fact that he is the only general in this campaign who understands the meaning of the events that are going on about him.

He alone understood the inactivity of the French army, he alone persistently declared that the battle of Borodino was a victory for the Russians. He alone used all his power to restrain the Russian army from undertaking more battles, which would have been useless, although in his position as commander-in-chief he ought rather to have been disposed to favor hostile measures.

IX.

THE BATTLE OF TAROUTINO.

THE Russian army was directed on the one hand by Koutouzof and his staff, and on the other by the Emperor Alexander I., who was at St. Petersburg.

Before news of the abandonment of Moscow had reached St. Petersburg, the tsar had drawn up a detailed plan of war and sent it to Koutouzof for the latter's guidance. Although the plan was made with the understanding that Moscow was still in the hands of the Russians, it was approved by Koutouzof's staff and accepted as the basis of action.

Koutouzof, however, wrote to St. Petersburg that it was very difficult to carry out a plan made at such a distance from the field.

The only reply was more instructions from St. Petersburg aiming to solve difficulties, and, at the same time, inspectors charged to see

that the orders were carried out and to send
back reports. Moreover, changes took place
in the staff of the Russian army. Bagration
had been killed ; Barclay, considering himself
ill-treated, withdrew, and these two generals had
to be replaced.

They debated with the utmost seriousness
whether it would be better to put Mr. A in the
place of Mr. B and Mr. B in the place of Mr. C,
or, on the contrary, to put Mr. B in the place of
Mr. C and Mr. C in the place of Mr. A ; as if
one or the other of these appointments could
have any influence whatever on the progress of
events, aside from giving pleasure to Messrs.
A, B, and C.

Meanwhile, animosity between Koutouzof and
the chief of staff, Bennigsen, the presence of
the tsar's inspectors, and the changes that followed, favored party intrigues, which became
more active than ever.

Mr. A, by the most varied and intricate
combinations, was undermining the authority of
Messrs. B and C.

The object of their intrigues was the war
which they thought they were conducting,

while the campaign went on independently in its own way, without conforming at all to the plans of these gentlemen, but as a result of the real relations of the armies in motion. All these intersecting and conflicting plans represented in the higher spheres of authority the faithfully reflected image of what ought to be accomplished.

On October 14, Alexander I. wrote to Koutouzof the following letter, which was received by the commander-in-chief after the battle of Taroutino : —

"Prince Mikhail Ilarionovitch ! —

"Since September 14, Moscow has been in the hands of the enemy. Your latest reports are dated October 2, and in all this time you have not only done nothing to deliver the first capital, but since your last reports you have been continually in retreat. Serpoukhov is already occupied by the enemy, and Toula, with its celebrated arsenal so necessary to the army, is in danger.

"By General Wintzengerod's report, I see that a body of the enemy, composed of ten thousand soldiers, is moving towards St. Petersburg; another body of several thousand men is marching upon Dmitrovo; a third is advancing on the road to Vladimir; a fourth, also large, is between Rouza and Mozhaïsk; and Napoleon himself was on October 7 at Moscow. . . .

"When, as appears from this information, the enemy has scattered his forces in considerable detachments, and Napoleon himself remains at Moscow with his Guard, is it possible that the strength of the enemy is still too great to prevent you from taking the offensive ? One might assume, with a conviction amounting to certainty, that you would pursue one or the other of these detachments, which are at least by an army corps weaker than the army which you command.

"It seems as if you would have profited by these circumstances to attack with advantage an enemy weaker than yourself, and either exterminate him, or at least oblige him to retire, thereby regaining the greater part of the territory now occupied by the enemy, and at the same time averting the danger which menaces Toula and the other towns of the interior.

"Upon you the responsibility will fall if the enemy succeeds in sending a considerable body of troops to St. Petersburg, and threatening the capital, which is almost destitute of soldiers; for, with the army which has been confided to you, if you act firmly and quickly, you have all the resources necessary to overcome these new evils.

"Remember that you must justify yourself before the country, which feels as an outrage the loss of Moscow!

"I have already proved my good-will towards you. This good-will shall not grow less, but I and Russia have a right to demand from you all the zeal, all the fortitude, and all the success that your mind, your military talents, and the courage of the troops which you command do not fail to assure."

But while this letter, which shows us the state of things as seen from St. Petersburg, was still on its way, Koutouzof could no longer restrain the army which he commanded, and which desired to take the offensive. They gave battle. On October 14, a Cossack, Shapovalof, while on patrol duty, shot at a rabbit, and, entering the woods in pursuit of the wounded animal, stumbled upon the unguarded left flank of Murat's army.

The Cossack, on his return to camp, laughingly told his comrades how he had fallen into the hands of the French ; a cornet, overhearing this, related what he had heard to his commander. The latter sent for the Cossack and questioned him.

The Cossack chiefs wished to profit by this opportunity and seize the enemy's horses ; but one of them who was in communication with headquarters told the chief of staff what had occurred.

At this moment, the relations of the staff were in the most strained condition.

Several days before, General Ermolof had sought out Bennigsen and implored him to use all his influence with Koutouzof in favor of assuming the offensive.

" If I did not know you," was Bennigsen's reply, " I should think that you were asking me something with the hope that it would not be

granted; I have only to advise Koutouzof to
do a thing to induce him to do exactly the contrary."

The news brought in by the Cossacks being
confirmed by a reconnaissance, it became evident that the time was ripe for action.

The strained cord broke. The hour of fate
had struck. The die was cast.

In spite of his fictitious power, his spirit, his experience, and his knowledge of men, Koutouzof,
— taking into consideration Bennigsen's reports
to the tsar, the desire expressed by the majority
of his generals, and the supposed wishes of the
tsar himself; knowing that he was powerless
to restrain longer a movement that was inevitable — gave the order for an attack which he
regarded as useless and harmful, and by so doing lent his approval to an accomplished fact.

Bennigsen's memoir addressed to the tsar,
and the stories of the Cossacks who blundered
on to the left flank of the French army, were
only the final indications of a necessity which
from day to day had forced the order for attack.
The Russians took the offensive on the 17th of
October.

The result of the battle was far from what had been hoped, and displeased everybody.

"That's the way things always go with us, always contrary to what has been expected!" the Russian generals said to each other after the battle; just as they say the same thing to-day to make us understand that there is always some imbecile to thwart their efforts, while, "we would have acted very differently."

Those who talk in this way do not know what war is or else they voluntarily deceive themselves.

Every battle, whether Taroutino, Borodino, or Austerlitz, goes on in a different way from the suppositions of the participants. This is a condition essential to war.

Innumerable and uncontrollable forces, — for nowhere is man more uncontrollable than in battle, where the question for each is that of life or death, — these uncontrollable forces, which influence the progress of the battle, can never be foreseen and can never be governed by a single guiding power.

When several different forces act at the same time upon any given body, the direction in

which the body moves will not be that of any
one of the forces, but will be a middle course,
as is demonstrated in mechanics by the diagonal
in the parallelogram of forces.

If, in the accounts of historians, and especially in those of French historians, we see
that wars and battles are invariably carried out
in accordance with plans made in advance, the
only conclusion that I can come to in regard to
these historians is that their descriptions are
not true.

The battle of Taroutino did not justify the
ideas of Toll, who wanted to put the troops in
action in proper order and in conformity to
predetermined dispositions; it did not meet
the expectations of Count Orlof, who wanted to
make Murat prisoner; it did not attain the end
proposed by Bennigsen and others, and destroy
the enemy at a single blow, that of officers who
went into the fight to win personal distinction,
or that of the Cossacks who were eager for
booty, — etc.

But if the principal aim of the attack, an aim
justified by what took place, was to carry out
the wishes of the Russian people, expel the

enemy from Russia, and exterminate his army, — then it is evident that the battle, because of its very incoherence, was just the battle necessary at this part of the campaign.

It is impossible to imagine as the issue of this battle a result more favorable to the final object of the campaign than the result which actually ensued.

With very little effort, and, in spite of a serious lack of system, very small losses, the Russians obtained the most important results achieved during the entire campaign; they passed from the defensive to the offensive, they laid bare the weakness of the French, and they gave to the French army a shock that sufficed to drive it into retreat. --

X.

NAPOLEON AT MOSCOW.

NAPOLEON enters Moscow after a brilliant victory; he cannot doubt the success of his arms, for the French remain masters of the field of battle.

The Russians retreat and give up their capital. Moscow, stored with provisions, arms, and riches innumerable, falls into the hands of Napoleon.

The Russian army, twice as weak as that of the enemy, passes an entire month without being able to assume the offensive.

Napoleon's situation is certainly brilliant. And whether he falls upon the remains of the Russian army and exterminates it with his doubly superior forces; or whether he decides to offer terms of peace, and, if his offer is rejected, to move upon St. Petersburg, returning, in case of unsuccess, to Smolensk or Vilna;

or whether he is contented with retaining the excellent position which he already occupies, — to me it seems that the choice of any one of the courses I have suggested does not demand any extraordinary display of genius.

It was only necessary to take the simplest and easiest way; not to allow the army to engage in pillage, to prepare clothing for winter (there was enough in Moscow for the whole army), and to get together the provisions, which, as French historians affirm, were of such great quantity that they would have sufficed to supply the French troops for at least six months.

And yet Napoleon, this genius of geniuses, who had, historians tell us, unlimited control of his army, did nothing of the sort.

He did nothing of the sort; but he used his power in favor of measures which were of all possible measures the most stupid and the most disastrous.

Of all the plans he might have chosen, — to pass the winter at Moscow, to move upon Nishnei-Novgorod, to return from north to south following Koutouzof, — it is impossible, I say, to imagine any plan more stupid or more disastrous than that actually chosen by Napoleon.

This was the plan : To remain in Moscow till the month of October, allowing his soldiers to pillage the city ; and then to emerge from Moscow, after considering whether or not to leave a garrison behind him, to approach Koutouzof without giving battle, to move to the right as far as Malo-Yaroslavetz, without considering the possibility of making a route of his own ; finally, instead of taking the course followed by Koutouzof, to withdraw toward Mozhaïsk through a devastated country. Once more I declare the impossibility of devising a plan more absurd in itself or more pernicious to the army. The assertion is fully proved by the results.

I defy the ablest master of strategy to invent a plan which would have led the French army to destruction (independently of any action on the part of the Russian army) as infallibly as did that selected by Napoleon.

Yes, the genius of Napoleon was guilty of this blunder. But to say that the emperor led his army to destruction because he wished to

destroy it, or because he was very stupid,
would be as false and as unjust as it would be
to say that Napoleon led his troops to Moscow
because he wished to do so and because he
was a man of genius.

‑In both cases, his personal action, which was
of no more consequence than the personal
action of any other soldier, only coincided with
the laws of the progress of events.

Because the events that followed did not
justify Napoleon, historians say that his intellectual powers had grown weaker at Moscow.
This assertion is erroneous.‑

Napoleon at Moscow made use of all his
intellectual power and all his knowledge to
defend his own interests and those of his army
in the best possible way, as he had always done
before, and as he did afterwards, in 1813. Bonaparte's action at this period of his life was not
less remarkable than it was in Egypt, in Italy,
in Austria, and in Prussia.

We do not know sufficiently well the real
condition of his genius in Egypt, "where from
the summit of the pyramids forty centuries"
looked down upon his greatness, for all his

great exploits there were recorded exclusively by French historians.

Neither can we rate at its proper value his action in Austria and in Prussia, for with regard to these two countries we must draw our information from French and German sources; and in a country where army corps surrender without striking a blow, and forts yield without a siege, Napoleon's genius would naturally be exalted as an explanation of a victorious campaign.

But we Russians have no reason for acknowledging the genius of Napoleon. We have no shame to hide. We have paid dearly for the right to consider facts as they are, and this right we will yield to no one!

The conduct of Napoleon at Moscow was as astonishing as it was anywhere else. From the time that he entered the capital, he did not cease to issue order upon order and to make plan upon plan. The absence of the inhabitants and of deputations, even the burning of the city, did not trouble him at all. He forgot nothing, neither the welfare of his army, nor the acts of the enemy, nor the good of the

Russian people, nor the administration of
affairs at Paris, nor diplomatic combinations in
the event of a possible peace.

In his purely military capacity, Napoleon, as
soon as he has entered Moscow, gives strict orders to General Sebastiani to watch the movements of the Russian army ; then he sends
troops in all directions, and orders Murat to
pursue Koutouzof.   At the same time, he forti-
fies the Kremlin, and traces upon the map of
Russia a plan for a future campaign.

Napoleon the diplomatist sends for Captain
Yakovlef, who had been despoiled of his command, and had been unable to get away from
Moscow.   To him Napoleon expounds his
political views, with the utmost magnanimity,
and then writes a letter to the Emperor Alexander, informing his " brother and friend " that
Rostoptchin has behaved very badly at Moscow ; and he sends Captain Yakovlef to St.
Petersburg to deliver this message to his sovereign.   Napoleon expresses the same ideas and
shows the same magnanimity to Toutolmin ;
and sends also this aged person to St. Petersburg to enter into negotiations with the tsar.

As the exponent of military law, Napoleon, after the conflagration, gives orders that the in-cendiaries shall be hunted down and put to death; and then, to punish the malefactor Rostoptchin, orders his houses to be set on fire.

As administrator of public affairs, Napoleon grants a constitution to Moscow, organizes a municipal government, and issues the following proclamation : —

INHABITANTS OF MOSCOW!

"Your miseries are great, but His Majesty the Emperor and King desires to put an end to your sufferings.

" Terrible examples have shown you how he punishes dis-obedience and crime. Severe measures have been taken to put an end to disorder and to restore general security.

" A paternal administration, composed of men chosen from among you, will govern your municipality. The administra-tive body will care for you, your needs, and your interests.

"The members of this municipal government will be dis-tinguished by a red scarf, which they will wear in form of cross; the mayor will wear beside the scarf a white belt.

" But when not on service, the members of the municipal government will wear simply a red band upon the left arm.

" The municipal police is instituted in conformity to its ancient organization, and thanks to its vigilance the best of order already reigns.

" The government has named two general commissioners, or *policemeisters*, and twenty magistrates, or *tchastni pristavs.*

assigned to different portions of the city. You will recognize them by a white band worn upon the left arm.

" Several churches of different sects are open, and divine service is there celebrated without obstacle.

" Your fellow-citizens are daily returning to their houses, and orders have been given that they shall have the aid and protection due to their misfortune.

" Such are the means by which the government hopes to re-establish order and mitigate your misfortunes. But to attain that end, you must unite your efforts with theirs, you must forget, if possible, the evils that you have endured, you must cherish the hope of a less cruel destiny, you must be con-vinced that an inevitable and infamous death awaits all those who make any assault upon your lives or your property, and especially you must believe that your welfare will be cher-ished, for such is the will of the greatest and most just of all monarchs.

" Soldiers and citizens, of whatever nation you may be ! — re-establish public confidence, that source of happiness in every state, live as brothers, aid and protect one another, be united to oppose all criminal manifestations, obey the mili-tary and municipal authorities, and soon your tears will cease to flow."

With regard to the provisioning of the army, Napoleon gave orders for the troops to forage through the city to procure food ; he thought thus to assure both bread and soldiers for the future.

With regard to religion, Napoleon ordered that the popes should be restored to their churches, and the forms of worship be re-established.

As to trade and the provisioning of the army, he issued the following

PROCLAMATION.

"You, peaceable inhabitants of Moscow, tradesmen and workmen whom misfortunes have caused to flee from this city, and you, dispersed farmers, who through unfounded terror remain concealed in the fields,— take notice!

"Peace reigns in the capital, and order is re-established. Your compatriots leave their retreats without fear, knowing that they will be respected.

"Any violence shown to them or prejudicial to their property is immediately punished.

"His Majesty the Emperor and King protects them, and counts none as his enemies among you save those who disobey his orders.

"He desires to put an end to your sufferings, and restore you to your houses and families.

"Respond to his benevolent intentions, and come to us without fear.

"Inhabitants!

"Return with confidence to your dwellings. You will soon find means of subsistence.

"Tradesmen and sons of toil!

"Return to your labors: houses, shops, watchmen await you, and for your labors you will receive the wage which is your due.

"And you, finally, peasants, come out of your forests, where you have been crouching in fear; return boldly to your *isbas*, and be persuaded that you will find protectors in us.

"Great markets have been established in the city, where the peasants may bring all the surplus products of their lands.

"To assure the free sale of these products, the government has taken the following measures:

"1. From this day, peasants, farmers, and other inhabitants of the suburbs of Moscow, may without danger bring their products to Moscow, to the two markets established for the purpose — in Mokhovaia Street and in the Okhotni Riad.

"2. These products will be purchased at prices agreed upon between seller and buyer, but if he who sells thinks the price unjust, he has the right to take away his goods, and no one shall prevent him from doing so.

"3. For this reason, large detachments of soldiers will, on Sundays, Wednesdays, Tuesdays, and Saturdays, be placed in the principal thoroughfares to protect the carts and horses of the peasants.

"4. The same measures will be taken to protect the return of the peasants to their villages.

"5. Measures will be taken to re-establish the ordinary markets with as little delay as possible.

"Inhabitants of the city and villages, and you, tradesmen, workmen, to whatever nation you may belong!

"We urge you to follow the paternal wishes of His Majesty the Emperor and King, and to aid him in the establishment of the general welfare.

"Bring to his feet respect and confidence, and do not hesitate to unite yourselves with us."

To keep up the spirits of the troops and the inhabitants, reviews were constantly held and there was an incessant distribution of decorations. The emperor rode through the streets on horseback to comfort the inhabitants, and, in spite of his preoccupation with state matters, he visited in person the theatres established by his formal orders.

As for charity, that virtue which doth most become a king, Napoleon displayed it also to the utmost extent that could be expected of him.

By his direction the words *My Mother's House* were inscribed upon buildings devoted to public charity, and by this loving act he united filial sentiment with the grand virtue of a monarch.

He visited the Foundling Asylum, and, allowing his white hands to be kissed by the children saved by his care, he magnanimously conversed with Toutolmin.

Moreover, as we learn from the eloquent narrative of Thiers, Napoleon ordered that the sums due his troops should be paid in counterfeit Russian money manufactured by himself.

"Emphasizing the employment of these means by an act worthy of him and of the French army," says the author of *The Consu-*

late and the Empire, "he gave aid to those
who had suffered from the effects of the
fires.   But provisions being too precious to
be given to foreigners, the greater part of
whom were enemies, Napoleon preferred to
provide money, of which he had a supply
ready, and he distributed among them a quantity of paper rubles."

Finally, to maintain the discipline of the
army, he issued orders threatening with severe
punishment all infractions of the rules of the
service, and he intimated that pillaging ought
to be stopped.

But, strangely enough, all these arrangements and measures and plans, which were
not at all inferior to those usually taken under
similar circumstances, moved at random and
without meaning, like the hands of a clock no
longer connected with the mechanism behind
the dial.

The plan for the campaign — the plan of
which Thiers says "that the genius of Napoleon never imagined anything more profound,
more skilful, or more admirable," and which,
disputing the assertions of M. Fain, he proves

to have been devised, not on the 5th of October, but on the 15th of that month — this plan was never carried out, and could not be, for it had no basis whatever in reality.

It was useless to fortify the Kremlin; to accomplish this work it was necessary to destroy the mosque, as Napoleon called the Church of St. Basil. The mines placed under the Kremlin served only the personal desire of the emperor, who wished to see the edifice blown up when he had got outside of the city — in other words, it was like a child beating the floor upon which he had fallen and hurt himself.

During the retreat of the French army, a most unheard-of thing took place. Napoleon was constantly on the lookout for the enemy, whom he knew to be at his heels, although the French army had lost sight of the pursuing Russian army, numbering not less than sixty thousand men. According to Thiers, it was due to the ability of Murat — to his genius, if I mistake not — that the French performed that brilliant feat of arms by which they discovered, like a needle in a haystack, the sixty thousand men of the Russian army.

From the diplomatic point of view, all the declarations of magnanimity and justice made by Napoleon to Yakovlef and to Toutolmin were entirely without effect. Alexander I. did not receive these two ambassadors from Napoleon, and did not reply to the letters which they carried.

After the execution of the supposed incendiaries, the other half of Moscow burned as the first had done.

The establishment of a municipal government did not put an end to pillage, and was of service only to the municipal councillors, who, under the pretext of establishing order, plundered Moscow, and thought only of saving their own property.

As to religion, which he had conciliated so readily in Egypt by visiting a mosque, Napoleon discovered that matters did not go so easily in Moscow. Two or three popes whom the French soldiers unearthed wished to pay homage to the emperor, but, one of them, while conducting divine service, having been struck upon both cheeks by a French soldier, they renounced their project. This is the account the French commissioner gave of the manner in which he conducted his stewardship.

"The priest whom I had discovered and commanded to begin again saying mass cleared and closed the church ; that night they went again to force open the doors, smashed the locks, tore the books in pieces, and committed all sorts of disorders."

As far as the re-establishment of trade was concerned, the proclamation to workmen and laborers and to the peasants did not have any effect. The laborious artisans did not exist ; the peasants seized the commissioners who ventured outside the city with the proclamation, and put them to death.

With regard to amusements, the result did not justify Napoleon's efforts. The theatres that were established in the Kremlin and in the house of Posniakof were soon closed because the actors and actresses had been despoiled of all they possessed.

Even his charities did not bring forth the anticipated fruits. Good and bad assignats were so abundant that neither class was of any value. The French, in return for their booty,

would accept nothing but gold. The assignats
that Napoleon distributed among the unfortu-
nates with such unparalleled generosity were
worthless, and silver itself was discounted in
favor of gold.

But the most striking proof of the ineffi-
ciency of all these orders is the result of the
measures taken by Napoleon to put an end to
pillage and re-establish discipline. Here are
some of the reports made by the commanding
officers : " Pillage continues in the city. In
spite of the order that it shall be stopped,
order is not yet re-established, and there is
not a merchant in legitimate trade. Sutlers
alone venture to sell anything, and they are
objects of pillage."

Another report: "A part of my district
continues to be pillaged by soldiers of the
Third Corps, who, not content with taking
from the unhappy refugees the little that they
have, are even brutal enough to strike them
with their swords, as I myself saw in several
instances."

A third report : " There is nothing new; the
soldiers still continue theft and pillage."

On the 9th of October: "Theft and pillage continue. There is a band of robbers in our district, who ought to be put down by a strong guard."

On the 11th of October, the governor of Moscow wrote: "The emperor is greatly displeased that, in spite of his strict orders against pillage, detachments of marauders from the Guard are continually entering the Kremlin. In the Old Guard, disorder and pillage were renewed yesterday and to-day more decidedly than ever. The emperor sees with sorrow the chosen soldiers, whose duty it is to defend his own person, and who ought to give an example of obedience, carrying disobedience so far as to despoil cellars and warehouses stocked with stores for the army; others have fallen so low that they refuse to obey the sentinels, and revile and beat them.

"The grand marshal of the palace complains bitterly that, notwithstanding his reiterated command, the soldiers continue to perform the offices of nature in all the courts, and even under the windows of the emperor."

Every day passed by the army at Moscow

hastened its disorganization and its end. It was like a herd fleeing in disorder, and trampling under its feet the food that would have saved it from hunger.

And yet this army would not stir from Moscow.

Only when the convoys were seized by the Russians on the road to Smolensk, and the news of the battle of Taroutino came, panic seized the French troops, and they took to flight with the utmost haste.

The news of the defeat at Taroutino, received unexpectedly by Napoleon during a review, inspired in him, Thiers tells us, the desire to punish the Russians, and he gave the order to begin the retreat, in accordance with the demand of the whole army.

On leaving Moscow, the troops loaded themselves down with all the booty they could get together.

Napoleon also had his own treasure to take with him. Seeing the vehicles obstructing the route of the army, Napoleon, to adopt Thiers' expression, was seized with horror. But, with all his experience of war, he did not order the superfluous wagons to be destroyed, as he had done when they were approaching Moscow. He cast a glance over the coaches and calashes in which the soldiers were travelling, and said that it was well — that these vehicles would be useful for carrying provisions, the sick, and the wounded.

The situation of the army was like that of a wounded animal feeling death to be near and not knowing how to escape it.

To watch the manœuvres and the purposes of Napoleon and his army, from the time he entered Moscow to the destruction of his forces, is like watching the convulsions and the agonized struggles of a beast wounded to the death. Often the wounded animal, hearing the noise of footsteps, runs directly in front of the always advancing hunter, turns, and hastens its own end.

Napoleon, under the pressure of his army, acted in this way.

The noise of the defeat at Taroutino alarmed the wounded animal. It jumped directly into the line of fire ; ran toward the hunter, turned, fled, and, like all hunted animals, sprang suddenly backward by the most dangerous, the most difficult, but the best known road, the road of its former trail.

—We imagine Napoleon to have been the director of all these movements, just as the savages imagine the figure-head upon the prow of a vessel to be the power that moves it onward. Napoleon, throughout the whole of this campaign, was like a child seated in a carriage clasping the sides, and imagining it is he that makes the horses go.

XI.

THE RETREAT FROM MOSCOW.

FROM the moment when Koutouzof learned that the French had left Moscow, and were beating a retreat, until the very end of the campaign, he used all his power, finesse as well as persuasion, with the sole purpose of preventing his troops from taking the offensive, and of turning them aside from encounters and combats with an enemy who was already doomed.

Doktourof goes to Malo-Yaroslavetz, but Koutouzof is in no hurry, and simply gives the order to leave Kalouga, knowing that, in case of necessity, it will be easy to retire behind that town.

Koutouzof retires ; but the enemy does not wait for his retreat before beginning its flight in another direction.

Historians describe the clever way in which Napoleon turned upon Taroutino and Malo-Yaroslavetz, and indulge in all sorts of hy-

potheses about what would have happened if
Napoleon had been able to enter the rich provinces to the south.

Without taking into consideration the fact
that nothing prevented Bonaparte from entering the provinces in question, since the Russians had given him a free field, historians forget
that at this time no circumstance or person
would have been able to save the French army,
for it carried within itself the elements of its
own destruction.

Why did the army which had found at Moscow an abundance of provisions, and, instead of
keeping them, had scattered them under its
feet; the army which at Smolensk, instead of
gathering stores, had given itself up to pillage, — why did this army now turn toward
Kalouga, where it was sure to encounter a
Russian population similar to that of Moscow,
and the same dangers from fire ?

This army was no longer able to retrieve
itself. At Borodino and the pillage of Moscow
it gathered the seeds of decomposition.

The men of this so-called "Grand Army"
ran, like their leaders, they knew not whither;

and all, from Napoleon to the lowliest soldier, had but one desire, that of escaping from a situation which seemed to them without meaning and without end.

And so, when, at Malo-Yaroslavetz, Napoleon's generals held the semblance of a council, to discuss various projects, the last opinion offered, that of General Mouton, prevailed. This simple and single-minded soldier had discovered the thought of the whole army: they must get away as quickly as possible. No one, not even Napoleon, opened his mouth to protest against a necessity recognized by all.

But, although every one agreed that they must depart, they nevertheless felt the humiliation of flight. Some external impulse was needed to overcome this sentiment. The shock came in the form of what Frenchmen call "the ambush of the emperor."*

The day after the council, Napoleon, pretending to inspect his troops and examine the field of battle, rode to the outer lines, accom-

---

* *Le hourra de l'empereur* — referring to the cries uttered by Cossacks when making a sudden attack upon an unsuspecting enemy. — H. S.

panied by his staff of marshals and by his guard. Some Cossacks, circling about in search of plunder, swept down upon the emperor, and there can be little doubt that he was made prisoner.

...That love of booty which was the destruction of the French army, and which on this occasion, as at Taroutino, led the Cossacks to think only of pillage, saved Napoleon. The Cossacks paid no attention to the emperor, but devoted themselves to the spoils, and Napoleon had a chance to escape.

When the French saw that the "children of the Don" had been able to lay hold upon the emperor in the midst of his own army, it became clear to them that there was only one thing to be done — they must beat a retreat, by the shortest and best known road.

Napoleon at forty was large of paunch, and no longer felt his former agility and courage. He submitted to necessity, under the influence of the fright given him by the Cossacks, sided with General Mouton, and, as the historians put it, *gave the order* to begin the retreat along the road to Smolensk.

The fact that Napoleon accepted Mouton's proposition, and that the French troops began to retire, does not prove that the movement was due to Napoleon ; it simply proves that the causes which were pushing the army in the direction of Mozhaïsk had also their influence upon Napoleon himself.

When a man is on a journey he has always a destination in view. If a man undertakes to travel a distance of six hundred miles, it must be because he looks for something good at the end. He must anticipate a promised land, to have strength enough to pass over so long a distance.

When the French entered Russia, their promised land was Moscow ; but when they fled from Moscow, their promised land was the country whence they came. This country was far away, and when a man starts out on a journey of six hundred miles, he is sure to forget the end in view, and he looks for consolations along the way.

"To-day," he says, "I will go ten leagues, and then I will rest ; " and, although this stage of his journey is not much nearer to his ultimate destination, upon it he concentrates all his hopes and all his desires.

A man's aspirations are always amplified and increased by action.

To the French, returning over the familiar way to Smolensk, the final end in view — to get back each to his own house — was too far away, and all their desires and hopes, which had attained enormous proportions, centred upon Smolensk. They did not expect to find there many provisions or fresh troops; on the contrary, Napoleon and all the generals of the army knew very well that there was nothing to be found at Smolensk, but the limited perspective of this stage of the journey was the only thing that could give the soldiers the power to march and to endure the privations of the moment. Those who knew the truth and those who knew it not alike sighed for Smolensk as their promised land.

Once on the road, the French hurried toward this fictitious destination with a remarkable energy and a still more astonishing velocity. This energy arose not only from the idea of a common end to which they were attracted, but also from their enormous numbers. This great multitude, as if obedient to the physical law of attraction, drew to itself all isolated atoms. This compact mass of one hundred thousand men moved on in a single body like an individual.

Each one of the men, taken by himself, wished for but one thing — to fall into captivity, and so to be delivered from the horror and sufferings of a forced march. But the influence of the common impulse which bore them toward Smolensk carried each one in the same direction. An entire corps could not surrender to a single battalion, and, although the French profited by every convenient and honorable occasion that offered itself for separation from their fellows and submission to the Russians, such occasions were not always at hand.

The great numbers of the French and the rapidity of their march prevented them from surrendering, and made it not only difficult but impossible for the Russians to arrest a movement in which was concentrated the entire energy of so enormous a mass.

The mechanical disruption of the body could not, beyond a certain limit, hasten the process of decomposition which was already in progress.

It is impossible to melt a snowball in an instant. There is a certain limit of time during which no degree of heat will be able to melt the snow. On the contrary, the greater the heat, the more solidified is the snow which remains.

With the exception of Koutouzof, none of the Russian generals understood what was going on. When they heard of the retreat of the French army on the road to Smolensk, they began to realize the truth of what Koutouzof had foreseen on the night of October 11. All the leading generals of the army wished to distinguish themselves, wished to bar the road of the French, to take them prisoners, to accelerate their flight; all were hot for pursuit.

Koutouzof alone employed all his powers, and those of a commanding general are not very great, to resist this idea of an offensive movement.

He could not say to his staff what we can

say to-day — why fight battles, why lose your own men and rush ferociously out to kill unfortunate wretches who will find death without your aid? why so much effort, when from Moscow to Viasma, without any combat whatever, a third of their army has disappeared?

Koutouzof could not use this language to his generals, but, giving them from his wisdom what he supposed they could understand, he said, " Give the enemy every chance ; it is the surest way of destroying him ; " but they mocked him, calumniated him, and, boasting and exulting, they hurled themselves upon the expiring animal to rend it and cut it in pieces.

At Viasma, Generals Ermolof, Miloradovitch, Platof, and others, finding themselves near the French, could not restrain themselves from cutting off the retreat of two army corps, and they derided Koutouzof by sending him a sheet of blank paper in lieu of a report.

In spite of Koutouzof's efforts to restrain his army, his troops assailed the French, and endeavored to bar their way. We are told that regiments of infantry, led by bands of music, advanced to the attack, and killed thousands of men without losing one of their own number.

And yet they could not check the fugitives, they could not exterminate the enemy. The French army drew its ranks more closely together, because of the danger, and advanced with undiminished velocity along this fatal road which led to Smolensk.

XII.

THE VICTORIES AND WHAT FOLLOWED.

THE battle of Borodino, followed by the occupation of Moscow, and finally by the retreat
of the French army without the intervention
of another battle, is one of the most instructive
events in history.

Historians agree that the external action of
states and peoples, when their interests conflict,
is expressed by war. They have many times
recorded the fact that after successes or re-
verses of arms the power of states and peoples
has increased or diminished.

It seems strange, on reading the story of a
war, to find such a king or such an emperor
getting his troops together, attacking the enemy's army, winning a victory, killing three
thousand, five thousand, ten thousand men, and
for this reason vanquishing a whole state com-
prising a population of millions of men. It is
hard to understand why the defeat of an army

— the loss of a hundredth part of a people's forces — should involve the submission of the entire people. And yet the facts of history, as they are taught to us, confirm the justice of the assertion that the success in arms of any people at war with another is the cause, or at least the true sign, of its own increase in power, and of decreased power on the part of the enemy.

When troops have won a victory, the powers of the victorious people are extended to the detriment of the vanquished. When troops have been beaten, the loss of power on the part of the people is proportionate to the defeat ; and when the troops have been entirely conquered, the people are completely vanquished.

This is the lesson that history teaches us, from the most ancient to the most recent times. All of Napoleon's wars confirm its truth.

In proportion as the Austrian troops were beaten, Austria lost her power, while the strength of France increased and acted in new directions. The French victories at Jena and Austerlitz destroyed the independence of Prussia.

But in 1812 the French bore off the victory of Muskova, and even seized Moscow, and yet immediately after these triumphs, without the fighting of any more battles, Russia continued to to exist, and this victorious army of six hundred thousand men was exterminated, and with it the France of Napoleon. Try as we may to force the facts to accommodate themselves to the rules of history, no one can say that the battle-field of Borodino was won by the Russians, or that, after the occupation of Moscow, battles were fought that decimated Napoleon's army, — this is not possible.

After the victory of the French at Borodino, there was no general battle, there was not the least engagement of any importance ; and yet the French army perished. What does this fact signify ?

If such a thing had occurred in the history of China, we should have said that it was not a historical event.

This is the favorite ruse of historians when the facts do not agree with their theories.

If it was a question of a minor war, with inconsiderable forces on either side, we might have said that the event was an exception to the general rule.

But it took place under the eyes of our fathers ; it meant to them the life or death of their country, and this war was the most momentous of all the wars known.

That period in the campaign of 1812 extending from the battle of Borodino to the retreat of the French proves not only that a battle won is not always a source of conquest, but that it may not be even a sign of victory; this event shows us that the force which decides the destiny of peoples does not consist in conquerors, or in armies, or in battles, but in something entirely different.

French historians, describing the condition of the troops before they left Moscow, assure us that everything was in good order in the "Grand Army," excepting the cavalry, the artillery, and the wagon-trains ; moreover, forage was lacking for the horses and cattle.   There was no remedy for this evil, for the mouzhiks preferred to burn their hay rather than to give it to the French.

The victory won by the French did not lead

to the usual results, because the mouzhiks Karp, Vlass, and others who went to Moscow with wagons after the departure of the French in search of plunder, and who gave no proof of any heroic sentiment, yet refused to carry hay to Moscow; in spite of the money offered to them, they preferred to burn the hay rather than to have it used for the service of the enemy.

Imagine two men engaged in a duel with swords according to the rules of fencing. For a considerable time their swords meet and cross; then all at-once one of the duellists, feeling that he has been wounded, and realizing that the affair is not a joke, but that his life depends upon it, throws aside his sword, and, seizing the first stick that comes to hand, begins to administer blows with his cudgel to right and left.

Imagine, still further, that this man, who has had recourse to a method so simple and efficacious, is imbued with traditions of chivalry, and, wishing to conceal the truth, declares that he came out victor according to the rules of fencing. The confusion that would enter into his story can easily be understood.

The duellist who demands an encounter according to the rules of fencing is the French; his enemy, who throws away his sword and takes up a club, is the Russians; those who try to make the combat agree with the rules are the historians who have described the campaign in Russia.

With the burning of Smolensk the´ campaign in Russia took a form until then unknown in the art of war. There were only burnings of towns and villages, and battles followed by precipitous retreats.

The retreat after the victory of Borodino, the burning of Moscow, the pursuit of the marauders, the sequestrated provisions, the guerilla warfare, — all these things were contrary to the rules of military tactics.

Napoleon felt this, and, when he had made his entry into Moscow in accordance with the rules of the game, he discovered that the hand of his enemy held a club instead of a sword, and after that he did not cease to complain that the war, as conducted by Koutouzof and

Alexander I., was not conducted according to rule — as if there were any need of rules for killing men.

But in vain the French complain that the Russians do not conform to the rules of war; in vain the superior officers of the Russian army blush at this method of defence with the cudgel, and desire a position where they can fight according to rule, — quarte, tierce, and a clever thrust, — the mouzhik has raised his club in all its terrible and majestic power, and, caring nothing for good taste and the rules, with a stupid but efficacious simplicity, striking out instinctively, falls upon the enemy and beats him incessantly, until the army of the invaders has perished.

Honor to the people who did not do as the French did in 1813, when they saluted the enemy according to the rules of the game, and, holding out their swords with politeness and grace, gave them up to their magnanimous conqueror. Honor to the people who in days of misfortune did not stop to ask how others had acted in conformity to the rules in similar circumstances, but who simply and quickly

seized the first club at hand, and showered
blows upon the enemy with redoubled energy,
until the feeling of anger and vengeance that
filled their hearts gave place to contempt and
pity!

XIII.

THE SPIRIT OF THE TROOPS AND GUERILLA WARFARE.

ONE of the most obvious and advantageous infractions of the so-called rules of war is the action of isolated individuals against the strictly military combinations. This sort of action always occurs in wars of a popular character. Instead of meeting the enemy in a compact body, men disperse, attack separately, retire when they see themselves threatened by any considerable force, to reappear at the first favorable opportunity.

So fought the Guerillas in Spain, the Mountaineers in the Caucasus, and the Russians in 1812.

Warfare of this sort is called irregular or guerilla warfare and by speaking of it in these terms we explain its meaning.

This sort of warfare is not only at variance with the rules of military art; it is in contradiction to that infallible law of tactics which demands that the assailant shall concentrate his troops, and be at the moment of combat stronger than his enemy. Guerilla warfare, always successful, as history proves, is entirely opposed to that law.

The contradiction arises from the fact that military science judges the strength of troops by their numbers. Military science says : The more troops, the greater strength ; the great battalions are always right.

An assertion like this bases military science upon that theory in mechanics which, considering moving bodies only with reference to their masses, affirms that their forces of momentum will be equal or unequal as their masses are equal or unequal.

Now, momentum (the *quantity* of movement) is the product of the mass multiplied by the velocity.

In war the momentum of troops is the product of the mass multiplied by an unknown quantity, x.

Military science, discovering, from a great many examples in history, that the masses of troops do not correspond with the strength of armies, and that small detachments have conquered large ones, recognizes confusedly the existence of an unknown factor, which it tries to find now in geometrical combinations, now in differences of armament, but especially — because that seems to be the simplest way of all — in the genius of the commanders.

These values are given in vain to the factor in question ; the results are not in accordance with historical facts.

We must renounce the false idea, invented for the pleasure of heroes, that if the arrangements made by the commanders are carried out in the war, we shall find x.

X is the spirit of the troops, the more or less intense desire of all the men composing them to fight, independently of the fact whether they are under the command of a man of genius or an imbecile, whether they fight in two or three ranks, whether they are armed with clubs or with guns delivering thirty shots a minute.

- Men who are eager to fight always put themselves in the most advantageous position for the struggle. The spirit of the army is the factor which, multiplied by the mass, gives the product of power.

To determine and express the meaning of that unknown factor, the spirit of the army, is the duty of science.

The problem will be solved only when we stop putting in place of x the conditions of the moment, such as the dispositions of the commanders, the armament, and so on, and realize that x in all its integration is the more or less active desire animating the men to confront danger. Only then shall we be able to express known historical facts by means of equations, and so determine the unknown factor.

Ten men, or ten battalions, or ten divisions, fighting with fifteen men, or fifteen battalions, or fifteen divisions, conquer the latter, killing their enemies or taking them prisoners, losing themselves only four men, battalions, or divisions. One side has lost fifteen, the other four. This may be expressed in the following equation : —

$$4x = 15y ;$$

whence,

$$x : y :: 15 : 4.$$

This equation does not give the value of the unknown quantity, but it expresses the relations which the two unknown factors bear to one another, and, by putting into the form of similar equations different historical units,— battles, campaigns, periods of war,— we shall obtain a series of numbers from which we may no doubt discover laws.

The rule of tactics commanding troops to act together in an attack and separately in a retreat undoubtedly expresses the truth that the strength of troops depends upon their courage. Better discipline is required to lead men against bullets than to induce them to defend themselves against assailants, and is obtained exclusively by movements in mass.

But this rule, taking no account of the courage of the troops, is always relative and defective, and particularly so in popular wars, when it is always contradictory to the truth, because then the increased or diminished courage of the troops is most freely manifested.

So the French, in 1812, in beating a retreat, should, according to tactics, have defended themselves separately; but, as a matter of fact, they drew more closely together, for the spirit of the troops had fallen so low that it could only be maintained by the men in mass.

The Russians, on the contrary, ought, according to tactics, to have attacked in mass; but the fact is that they scattered their forces, because the spirit of their troops had reached such a point that isolated men attacked the enemy without waiting for a command, and had no need of encouragement or constraint to induce them to expose themselves to the fatigues and the perils of war.

XIV.

THE FLIGHT OF NAPOLEON.

WHEN freezing weather began, on November 8, the French retreat suddenly assumed a more tragic character. Men were frozen on the march, and others, seeking to warm their stiffened limbs at the bivouac fires, were literally roasted to death ; and, close by, the emperor and his retinue of kings and dukes rode along in carriages, wrapped in their furs, and bearing the treasures they had stolen. But the truth is that nothing could hasten or restrain the progress of flight or the decomposition of the French army after its egress from Moscow.

Without taking account of the Guard, which throughout the entire campaign gave itself over to pillage, we find that during the movement from the capital to Viasma the seventy-three thousand men of the French army were reduced to thirty-six thousand, and, of the number lost, only five thousand fell in battle.

This is the first term in a progression which indicates with mathematical precision the terms that are to follow.

The French army was destroyed and melted away in the same proportion from Moscow to Viasma, from Viasma to Smolensk, from Smolensk to Beresina, and from Beresina to Vilna, independently of the varying degree of cold, the pursuit of the enemy on its path, and of all other circumstances.

After Viasma, the French troops drew together in a single mass, and so continued to the end.

Although we know how far from the truth are reports made by generals on the condition of their troops, we read not without interest what Berthier wrote, at this time, to the emperor : —

" I think I ought to acquaint Your Majesty with the condition of the troops in the different army corps that have during the last two or three days come under my inspection.   They are nearly disbanded.   The number of soldiers following the standards is, at the most, less than a fourth in nearly all the regiments ; the others go by themselves in different directions,

in the hope of finding provisions and to escape from discipline. The majority of them look to Smolensk as the place
where they will recruit from their sufferings. During the last
few days, we have noticed many soldiers throwing away their
muskets and cartridges. In this condition of things, the interests of Your Majesty's service require that, whatever our ultimate plans, the army should be rallied at Smolensk, and the
ranks rid of non-combatants, of unmounted men, of useless
baggage, and of such artillery stores as are no longer actually
needed. Moreover, the soldiers require some days of rest and
supplies of adequate food, for they are worn out by fatigue and
hunger ; many in the last few days have died on the march or
in bivouac. As this state of things is constantly growing worse,
we begin to fear that, if remedies are not promptly applied,
we shall not be able to control the troops in case of battle. —
November 9, at thirty versts from Smolensk."

The French rushed into Smolensk, which
was to them like the promised land, fought
with one another for food, pillaged their own
stores, and when they had plundered everything within their reach, they hurried on.

They all fled, not knowing whither or why ;
and Napoleon, with all his genius, knew less
than others why they did so, for he was the
only one who fled without having received from
another a command to fly.

During the disordered retreat, he and his
underlings retain their former habits. They

write orders and reports, and they shower titles
upon one another, — Sire, My Cousin, Prince
of Eckmühl, King of Naples, etc. But these
orders exist only on paper; no one carries
them out, because they are no longer possible.
Napoleon and his family may continue to
address each other as Majesty, Highness,
and Cousin; they feel none the less that they
are miserable wretches, who have done an im-
mense amount of harm, and that their expiation
has begun. And, pretending to be very solici-
tous about the army, they think only of their
own skins, each making all possible efforts to
save his own little person.

The conduct of the Russian and French
troops during the retreat of the "Grand Army"
from Moscow to the Niemen reminds one of
the game of blind-man's-buff. Both players
have their eyes bandaged, and one of them is
provided with a bell, which he sounds from
time to time, to attract the attention of his adversary. At first, the one who is to be caught
sounds his bell without fear, but when he feels
that the pursuer is pressing him closely, he

seeks to evade his adversary by taking to his heels, and yet, at the moment when he thinks he is safe, he runs directly into the arms of his pursuer.

At the beginning of the campaign, Napoleon's troops, while on the road to Kalouga in the first period of their retrograde movement, give still some signs of life ; but once on the road to Smolensk, they seize the clapper of the bell in their hands, and run with all their speed, and, believing that they are making good their escape from the Russian troops, throw themselves directly in the way of the enemy.

The wild speed of French and Russians was too much for the horses, so that reconnaissance by cavalry, the best method of ascertaining the position of an enemy, became impossible. Moreover, the changes of position in both armies were so numerous and rapid that information always came too late.

News came on a certain day that the enemy's army was the night before at such and such a place, and on the morrow, by the time that anything could be done, they found that the army had already made a two-days march and had taken another position.

One army fled and the other followed. On leaving Smolensk, the French troops had a number of routes to choose from. It seems as if Napoleon and his generals, having made a four-days halt, might have occupied the time profitably by reconnoitring the enemy, and adopting different tactics. But, instead of this, after the four-days rest, the army moved on in mass, turning neither to the right nor to the left, but without reflection following their former route, the worst that was accessible, that of Krasnoë and Orsha.

Thinking always that the enemy was at their heels and not before them, the French hastened on, spreading out and dispersing their forces, so that some were often twenty-four hours march from the others.

At the head of the whole army ran the emperor; after him came the kings, and then the dukes.

The Russian army, believing that Napoleon would take the only reasonable route and turn to the right toward the Dnieper, themselves

turned to the right, and followed the main road
in the direction of Krasnoë.

At this point in the game of blind-man's-buff,
the French ran against the Russian advance
guard.

Having thus unexpectedly discovered the
enemy, they were confused, and paused an instant in astonishment and fright, only to resume
their course, abandoning their comrades in the
rear. There, for three days, the isolated fragments of the French army ran the gauntlet of
the Russian troops ; first came the corps of the
viceroy, then that of Davoust, finally that of Ney.

They abandoned their comrades, they abandoned half of their forces in their flight, lying
hid by day, and marching by night in a thousand détours and semicircles.

Ney, who came last, because he had stopped
to blow up the unoffending walls of Smolensk,
rejoined Napoleon at Orsha with one thousand
men out of the ten thousand who had been
under his command. Abandoning a part of his
soldiers and his artillery, he had succeeded in
slipping through the woods by night and in
crossing the Dnieper.

From Orsha they hastened on toward Vilna, still playing the game of blind-man's-buff with the pursuing enemy.

At Beresina the confusion increased. A great many men were drowned, others gave themselves up; but those who crossed the river still hastened on.

Napoleon, wrapped up in his furs, passed in a sledge, and, abandoning his companions in arms, escaped with all possible haste.

Those of his generals who could do so followed his example ; those who could not, surrendered or perished by the way.

During this period of the Russian campaign the leaders of the French army did everything that was possible to destroy their troops. As we follow the movement of this mass of men from the beginning of its march to Kalouga to the flight of Napoleon, we can find no indication of wisdom in the conduct of the army, — and it would seem that historians who make the action of the masses depend upon the will of a single man ought not to try to write the history of this campaign in any such way.

And yet they do. Historians without number have gravely discussed, in mountains of print, the plans and dispositions adopted by Napoleon in this campaign, and find them to be immeasurably profound ; they are in ecstasies over the manœuvres executed by the troops, and the genius manifested in the measures adopted by the marshals.

The retreat by Malo-Yaroslavetz, — that useless retreat by a devastated route, chosen by Napoleon when he might have taken another that would have led him into provinces where provisions were abundant, the route for which he neglected the parallel road followed later by the pursuing Koutouzof,—this retreat has found defenders, who vindicate it on the plea of superior tactics ; and these same superior tactics ought to explain the retreat from Smolensk to Orsha.

But the historians of Napoleon are not satisfied with vindicating their hero. They vaunt his bravery in putting himself at the head of his troops at Krasnoë, where he intended to give battle. They represent him marching on foot at the head of his army, with a cane in his hand, and saying : —

"Enough of the emperor ; it is time for the general."

—In spite of these fantastic stories, we find that he fled instead of fighting, leaving behind him the defenceless fragments of his army.

Sometimes the historians are pleased to exalt the grandeur of soul displayed by the marshals, particularly by Ney, who, in the grandeur of his soul, succeeded in getting through the forest by night, passing the Dnieper, and finally entering Orsha without colors, without artillery, and leaving behind him nine-tenths of his army.

—Finally, when the great emperor himself abandons his army, historians represent the act as something grand, a stroke of genius. This miserable flight, which we simple mortals look upon as a most scurvy act, which we teach our children to consider a shameful deed, this vile trick historians find means to justify.

For when their attenuated thread of logic will bear no more stretching, when the actions of their hero are in flagrant contradiction with what humanity calls good and right, the historians take refuge in the idea of greatness.

With them greatness excludes all idea of good
and evil. In him who is great, nothing is bad.
He who is proclaimed great is acquitted of all
the atrocities that he may have committed.

"He is great!" cry the historians; and
there is no more good or evil, there is only
what is "great" and what is not "great."

What is "great" is good, what is not is bad.

"Greatness" is with them the quality of certain beings set apart, whom they call heroes.

And Napoleon, fleeing to his own fireside,
warmly wrapped in his furs, and leaving behind
his companions in arms and that multitude
of men whom he had led into Russia, feels that
he has done something great, and his soul is
tranquil.

"There is only one step," he himself said,
"from the sublime" (he thinks himself sublime!) "to the ridiculous." And for fifty years
the universe has cried after him, "Sublime!
Great! Napoleon the Great!" Truly, there is
only one step from the sublime to the ridiculous!

They do not see that by taking greatness as
the standard of good and evil they thereby

declare the emptiness and littleness of what they call great.

For us there is no greatness where there is not simplicity or goodness or justice.

XV.

PURSUING THE FRENCH.

WHERE is the Russian who, reading the story of the last period of the campaign of 1812, has not experienced a profound feeling of vexation, discontent, and perplexity?

Who has not asked himself why we did not destroy or capture all the French, when they were surrounded by our three greater Russian armies; when, dying of hunger, they surrendered in crowds; and when, as history tells us, the proper aim of the Russians was to cut off the retreat of the French, to stop them, and to take them prisoners?

Why, if the proper object of this army, — which at first, less in number, fought the battle of Borodino and then surrounded the French on three sides, — if the true object of this army was to cut off the retreat of the French and take them prisoners, why did it not achieve the end in view?

Were the French so superior to the Russians that the latter, after having surrounded their enemy, considered themselves unequal to the conquest?

If such was the aim of the Russians, how was it that their plans miscarried?

History—or what is called history—replies to these questions by declaring that Russia did not attain the object in question because Koutouzof, Tormasof, Tchitchagof, and others did not execute such and such a manœuvre.

But why were not these manœuvres executed? If it was the fault of these generals that the end in view was not attained, why were they not court-martialled and put to death?

But even if we were to admit that Koutouzof and Tchitchagof were the cause of Russian "unsuccess," we should still find it impossible to understand why our troops, who were in superior force at Krasnoë and Beresina, did not disarm the French troops and seize the marshals, the kings, and the emperor, if such was the object of the Russians. We cannot explain this strange phenomenon—as do the

majority of military Russians — by saying that
it was because Koutouzof forbade our troops
from taking the offensive. Such reasons we
know to be specious, for we have seen that
Koutouzof was unable to restrain the troops
either at Viasma or at Taroutino.

If the object of the Russians was truly to cut
off the retreat of the French army and to take
Napoleon and his marshals captives, — since
this object was not attained, and since all
attempts in that direction were shameful fail-
ures, — the French were right in representing
the last period of the campaign as a series of
victories, and Russian historians are wrong
when they claim that we were victorious.

Russian military historians are, in spite of
their lyrical outbursts in regard to the courage
and patriotism of their countrymen, logically
forced to the conclusion that the retreat from
Moscow was for Napoleon a series of victories, and for Koutouzof a series of defeats.

But, if I put aside national pride, I discover
that this conclusion involves a contradiction,
for this series of victories on the part of Napoleon led the French to complete destruction,

and the series of defeats endured by Koutouzof led the Russians to the overthrow of the enemy and the elutriation of their territory.

The source of this contradiction lies in the fact that historians study events in the correspondence of kings and generals, and by means of official narratives and reports, and they have assumed that the object of the last period in the campaign of 1812 was to cut off the retreat of the French and to seize Napoleon and his marshals.

This object did not exist at all, and could not exist, because it would have been foolish, and it would have been impossible of attainment.

_ The object would have been foolish, in the first place, because Napoleon's defeated army was flying from Russian territory with all possible speed, and thereby fulfilling the wishes of all Russians. Why direct military operations against an enemy who is running away as fast as he can go?

Secondly, it would have been foolish to try to stop men who were employing all their energy in the effort to get away with all possible celerity.

Thirdly, it would have been foolish to sacrifice men in fighting an enemy who was destroying himself by contact with external causes, and that at such a rate that even with an open road the French could carry to the frontiers only the small number that remained to them in the month of December — a hundredth part of all their forces.

Fourthly, it would have been foolish to make prisoners of the emperor, the kings, and the marshals, for their captivity would have been exceedingly embarrassing to the Russians, as De Maistre and other able diplomatists of the time clearly recognized.

It would have been still more foolish to capture whole regiments of Frenchmen, when the Russian army had been depleted one-half by the time it got to Krasnoë, and entire divisions would have been needed to guard the prisoners. How could they have cared for prisoners when the Russian soldiers were not receiving full rations and when the French were dying of cold and hunger?

This profound plan of seizing Napoleon and his army reminds one of the gardener who, instead of driving away the animal that was ravaging his borders, ran behind the gate to crush it when it passed out. The only thing one can say in his favor is that he was no longer master of himself in his wrath. Not even this excuse can be made for those who devised the plan of seizing Napoleon and his staff, for they were not the ones who had to bear the damage done to the ravaged borders. —The idea of cutting off the retreat of Napoleon and his army was not only foolish — it was impossible.

First, because, as experience shows, the movement of columns of soldiers in battle for a distance of thirty miles can never be made in accordance with a prearranged plan. It was more than improbable, it was impossible, that Generals Tchitchagof, Koutouzof, and Wittgenstein should effect a junction at a certain place at a certain time. Koutouzof understood this, and, when this plan of action was submitted to him, he objected that operations at great distances never gave the anticipated results.

Secondly, to overcome the momentum of Napoleon's army in its homeward flight, forces much greater than those possessed by Russia would have been necessary.

Thirdly, we use a foolish military phrase when we speak of "cutting off" an enemy. We may cut off a piece of bread, but not an army.

To cut off an army, to bar its road, is an impossible thing, for there are always chances for détours, and it is favored by night and obscurity, as military strategists may convince themselves if they will study what took place at Krasnoë and Beresina.

It is no more possible to seize a person who will not be seized than it is to seize a swallow unless it comes and lights upon your hand.

Armies can be made prisoners only when they do as the German army did, and surrender according to the rules of strategy and tactics. The French troops did not adopt this plan, for death by cold and hunger awaited them alike in flight and in captivity.

Fourthly, — and this is the most important consideration of all, — never since the world began was a war carried on under more terrible conditions than those which attended the campaign of 1812; and the Russian troops, by concentrating their efforts for the pursuit of the French, could do nothing more unless they incurred the penalty of annihilation.

During the movement of the Russians from Taroutino to Krasnoë, fifty thousand men, equivalent to half the population of an ordinary city, left the ranks — some sick, others disabled.

The Russian army, in this manner, lost half of its men without giving battle.

How have the historians described this period of the campaign, when the soldiers, without boots or great-coats, with insufficient food, and deprived of brandy, passed the nights in the snow, in a temperature fifteen degrees below freezing? The days then were only seven or eight hours long, and in the darkness that intervened discipline was impossible. In this way, men passed whole months between life and death, fighting against cold and hunger, not for a few hours, but incessantly, enduring privations so bitter that half of the army melted away in a single month.

And yet this is the period of the campaign that historians pretend to describe when they tell us how Miloradovitch ought to have made a flank movement în one direction, and Tormasof in another, and Tchitchagof in a third (the snow being knee-deep), and how such and such a general once cut off and destroyed an enemy's army! — and so on, and so on.

The Russians, of whom one-half had perished in the snow, accomplished all that they could or ought to do to attain an end worthy of the Russian people. It is not their fault if other Russians, with idle hands, in comfortably heated apartments, devised plans that could not be carried out.

All the strange contradictions between the historical facts and the account of the event as recorded in history, incomprehensible as they are to-day, arise simply from this : the historians who have told the story have given us, instead of facts, fine sentiments and the fine speeches of different generals.

To them, the most important incidents in this part of the campaign are the speeches of Miloradovitch, the plans of some other general, and the decoration of another; for the fifty thousand Russian soldiers who were left behind in hospitals, or who perished in the snow, historians feel no interest; the subject is outside of their jurisdiction.

And yet if the historians will only turn their attention to the reports and plans of the generals, they will be able to follow the movements of the hundred thousand soldiers who took an active part in what was going on, and all the questions that have troubled them so much will be solved at once.

The idea of cutting off the retreat of Napoleon and his army had no existence except in the imaginations of a dozen plan-makers. The idea could not be taken seriously, because it was as absurd as it was impracticable.

The Russian people had only one object in view, and that was to rid their soil of the invaders.

The object was attained, firstly, because the French abandoned Russia of their own accord, and it was only necessary that their flight should not be checked; secondly, because of the guerilla warfare, which decimated the

French army ; and, thirdly, because the greater part of the Russian army followed the enemy step by step, ready to resort to force if the French had suspended their flight.

The action of the Russian army was like the crack of a whip behind an animal already under full headway.

An experienced cattle-driver knows that the most efficacious method of hastening the speed of an animal is to threaten it with upraised whip, but not to strike.

. . . .

XVI.

KOUTOUZOF.

AFTER the encounter at Viasma, which took place because Koutouzof could no longer restrain the impetuosity of his troops, who wished at any price to " sweep away," to " cut off," to "hold back," the French army, the subsequent retreat to Krasnoë, during which time the French had the Russians at their heels, took place without the occurrence of a battle. The progress of the French was so rapid that the Russians could not keep up with them, and lost them from view; their horses in the cavalry and artillery were unequal to the advance, and they were only imperfectly informed in regard to the movements of the enemy. The Russian soldiers, worn out by daily marches of forty versts, could no longer press onward.

To understand what this army endured from fatigue, we have only to remember that the

Russian army, on leaving Taroutino, numbered one hundred thousand men, and that although they lost, aside from a hundred or so taken prisoners, not more than five thousand in killed and wounded, they had only fifty thousand men when they got to Krasnoë.

The breathless pursuit of the Russian army was as disastrous on the one hand as was the precipitous retreat of the French army on the other. The only difference in their respective conditions was that the Russian troops marched at will without being exposed to attack ; the French troops advanced under a menace of certain destruction, knowing that their sick would fall into the hands of the enemy; while the Russians who could no longer endure the fatigue of the campaign were able to return to their homes.

The principal cause of the diminution of the French army was the rapidity of its flight, as we see by comparing its losses with those of the Russian army launched in pursuit.

Koutouzof restricted his efforts, as he had done at Taroutino and Viasma, to the prevention of any interference with the destructive

progress of the French, although this was contrary to directions from St. Petersburg and the
opinion of his own generals. His only desire
was to facilitate the course that the enemy had
chosen, and to make the march of his own
troops as easy as possible.

Moreover, when Koutouzof saw the signs of
fatigue manifested by his army, and the losses
it had undergone, he found another reason for
slackening his pursuit of the enemy and waiting to see what would happen. They did not
know what route would be taken by the
French, who made greater speed the more
closely they were pressed by the Russian soldiers. Only by following at a distance could
the Russians avoid the zigzags of the enemy
and pursue them by the most direct road.

The intricate manœuvres proposed by the
other generals involved an increase in the daily
marches, while the only reasonable course to
pursue was to reduce the marches as much as
possible.

Toward this latter object all the efforts of
Koutouzof were directed from Moscow to
Vilna ; the pursuit was not to him a matter of

accident or caprice, but he maintained it with a persistency and perseverance that did not for a moment relax.

These tactics were dictated to Koutouzof, not by science and reason, but by his heart. That truly Russian heart knew and felt what every Russian soldier knew and felt, that the French were vanquished, and that, to be rid of them forever, it was only necessary to provide them with an escort to the frontier; and at the same time he felt with his soldiers the grievous weight of a campaign made terrible by the rapidity of the marches and the intensity of the cold.

But the other generals, principally those who were not Russian at all, wanted to distinguish themselves, to astonish the world, to take a king prisoner, or at least a duke; their only idea was to give battle and conquer, although a battle would have been odious and absurd.

When they brought their plans for battles to Koutouzof, he looked at his soldiers, famished, without shoes, without great-coats, who had been for a month without fires, reduced

to half their former numbers, and with whom
he must pursue the enemy a distance greater
than that already traversed, to the frontier,—
Koutouzof saw this, and his reply to the generals who wanted to distinguish themselves
was simply a shrug of the shoulders.

The desire to display bravery, to direct manœuvres, to harass the enemy, was especially
manifested when the Russian troops encoun-
tered a detachment of the French army. That
was the case at Krasnoë, where the Russian
generals, believing themselves confronted by
two or three columns of the French army,
hurled themselves upon Napoleon and his sixteen thousand men.

In spite of Koutouzof's efforts to avoid this
engagement and to save his troops, the Russians for three days kept up an indiscriminate
attack on the French stragglers.

Colonel Toll, a German, prepared a plan, in
which he says, "*die erste Colonne marschirt,* the
first column will march, etc." And, as always
happens, everything went on contrary to the
plan.

Prince Eugene of Würtemberg saw from a

hill-top a number of French on the road, and
asked for re-enforcements, which did not arrive.
That night the French turned the Russian
position, scattered through the woods, and re-
sumed their march as best they could.

General Miloradovitch, who declared that he
had nothing to do with the provisioning of his
troops, and that he cared nothing whatever
about it, who could never be found when he
was wanted, who called himself a "chevalier
without fear and without reproach," had a
weakness for French conversation, and was
always talking with the French, proposing
terms of surrender, and so losing a great
deal of time without executing the orders
intrusted to him.

"I make you a present of that column,
my children," he said to his troops, pointing
to the French.

And his troops, mounted upon worn-out
horses, urged their steeds with spur and
sword-thrusts into a slow trot, and advanced
upon the column which the general had
given them. It was composed of a crowd of
poor Frenchmen already half-dead with hunger

and cold. This column, whose destiny had been so generously disposed of, threw down its arms and surrendered, a consummation which it long had wished.

At Krasnoë, these generals took twenty-one thousand Frenchmen prisoners, and captured hundreds of cannon and a bâton which they called "the marshal's bâton." They passed the time in a discussion as to who had distinguished himself the most, and they were entirely contented with themselves.

Their only regret was that they had not succeeded in seizing Napoleon, or at least one of the marshals, and they reproached one another about it, and complained of it to Koutouzof.

These men, carried away by their passions, were only the agents of sad necessity, but they believed themselves to be heroes, and imagined that they had accomplished a most noble and worthy work.

They blamed Koutouzof for having prevented them, since the beginning of the campaign, from vanquishing Napoleon, and for thinking only of his own personal predilections, and they added that he refused to leave Polotniani Zavodi because he was contented with his position there. Finally, they maintained that he had stopped the movements of the troops at Krasnoë because he had lost his head in the presence of Napoleon, even going so far as to accuse him of an understanding with Napoleon, of allowing himself to be bought over, etc.[1]

Koutouzof was not only condemned by prejudiced contemporaries, but posterity and history, which proclaim Napoleon "great," see in Koutouzof only an old, weak, cunning, and debauched courtier; thus is he regarded by foreigners, while Russians look upon him as an indefinite sort of person, a marionette, who was useful only because he bore a Russian name.

In 1812–1813, Koutouzof was openly accused of having made serious mistakes.

Alexander I. was displeased with him, and in the history of the campaign recently written by imperial order,[2] Koutouzof is represented

---

[1] Wilson's Memoir.

[2] History of 1812, by Bogdanovitch; accounts of Koutouzof, and dissertation on the insufficient results attained at the battle of Krasnoë.

as a lying and crafty courtier, who trembled
at the very name of Napoleon, and who, by
the errors he committed at Krasnoë and Beresina, deprived the Russian arms of a complete
victory over the French.

Such is the fate of mortals who are not *great
men,* — or, as the Russian mind never recognizes great men, let us say that such is the
fate of those rare and nearly always isolated
souls who are able to penetrate the designs of
Providence and subordinate their own wills.

The hatred and scorn of the multitude is the
punishment these men have to endure for their
ability to understand superior laws.

To Russian historians (what a strange and
horrible thing to say !), Napoleon, that vile in-
strument of history, who never anywhere, not
even in exile, displayed the dignity of manhood, — this man is the object of admiration
and enthusiasm : he is great !

Koutouzof, the man who from the beginning
to the end of the campaign of 1812, from Borodino to Vilna, did not once, by a single act or
a single word, deviate from his plan, but who
presented one of the rarest examples of self-

sacrifice and insight,— Koutouzof is nothing to the Russian historians, and when they speak of him, and of the great affairs of the year 1812, they are ashamed.

And yet it would be difficult to call to mind a historical personage whose activity has been so faithfully and so constantly devoted to a lofty aim — an aim which expressed all the aspirations of a people.

It would be equally difficult to discover in history another example of an object so completely realized as was that to which Koutouzof entirely devoted himself in 1812.

Koutouzof never talked about the forty centuries that looked down from the summit of the Pyramids ; he never spoke of the sacrifices he had made for his country, of the great things that he would accomplish or of those he had already done.

He never spoke of himself, never attempted to play a part, was careful to be like everybody else, to be always natural in his manners, and to say only the most simple and the most ordinary things.

He wrote letters to his daughters and to

Madame De Staël, read romances, enjoyed the society of beautiful women, and was on familiar terms with generals, officers, and soldiers. He never contradicted anybody who tried to convince him of anything.

When Count Rostoptchin rode with all speed across the Zhaousa bridge to join Koutouzof, and reproached him with the loss of Moscow, adding, —

"And yet you promised not to surrender Moscow without a battle,"

Koutouzof, knowing that Moscow was already abandoned, replied : —

"I shall not give up Moscow without a battle."

When Count Araktshïef, directed by the tsar, came to tell him that General Ermolof must be appointed commander-in-chief of the artillery, Koutouzof, although he had a few moments before declared himself against the appointment, replied : —

"I was about to propose it myself."

What mattered to him, to him who alone of all the foolish crowd about him understood the grandeur of events, what mattered to him the reproaches of Rostoptchin, or the question as to who should be named chief of artillery ?

Not only in circumstances similar to those that I have mentioned, but on all occasions, this old man, who by experience of life had learned with certainty that the thoughts and words of men are not related to their actions, spoke without meaning, saying whatever came into his head.

But this same man, who made light of speech on such occasions, did not, throughout the whole campaign, utter a word at variance with the object toward which he so resolutely moved.

It is evident that not wilfulness but a painful assurance that he would not be understood led him many times in different circumstances to conceal his thoughts.

After the battle of Borodino, when the misunderstanding between him and his staff began, he alone declared that *Borodino was a victory*, and he repeated it many times orally and in his letters, as well as in his reports, up to the time of his death.

He also was the only one to declare that *the loss of Moscow was not the loss of Russia.*

He it was who, in reply to Lauriston, sent by Napoleon to offer terms of peace, said that he could not make peace, because *the Russian people did not wish it.*

He alone, during the retreat of the French, declared that *all military operations were useless, that the affair would take care of itself in accordance with the wishes of the Russians, that it was only necessary to facilitate the progress of the enemy, that neither the battle of Taroutino nor that of Krasnoë nor that of Viasma was necessary, that they must spare their men if they wished to reach the frontier with any troops, and finally that he would not sacrifice the life of a single Russian soldier even to make ten prisoners.*

And it was he, the man who is represented as a deceitful courtier, who at Vilna said to the tsar, at the risk of disgrace, that *to continue the war beyond the frontier would be useless and dangerous.*

But words alone would not prove sufficiently that he grasped the full progress of events.

All his acts, all his deeds, all his achievements tended to one object, from which he was not for one moment turned aside, and which he sought to obtain by three methods : —

1. Concentrating all his forces in view of an encounter with the French.

2. Vanquishing them.

3. Driving them from Russia while incurring the least possible suffering on the part of the Russian troops and the Russian people.

It was Koutouzof the temporizer, the man whose device was "patience and plenty of time," who gave battle at Borodino, and who made the preparations for that battle with unexampled solemnity.

It was Koutouzof who, before hostilities began at Austerlitz, declared that the battle was lost ; and concerning Borodino, where all the generals acknowledged defeat, protested, up to the time of his death, that the battle had been won by the Russians, although a victory followed by retreat had never before been known to history.

Finally, as we have seen, he was the only one during the retreat who declared that any more battles were useless, and who opposed the idea of crossing the frontier to begin a new war.

If we no longer confound the wishes of the masses with plans fermenting in the heads of a dozen ambitious upstarts, we shall be able distinctly to see the great event which is now in all its completeness spread before our eyes.

How was it that this old man, alone against many, divined with so much perspicacity the national import of events, and did not once contradict himself throughout the whole campaign?

This power of insight had its source in the sentiment of the Russian people, which was carried by Koutouzof in his heart with undiminished purity and vigor.

And because the Russian people recognized this sentiment in Koutouzof, they chose the old man, disgraced as he was at court, to be the leader in the national war, chose him against the will of the tsar.

This sentiment, and nothing else, elevated Koutouzof to the height of human feeling,

and led him, the general in command, to
employ all his efforts, not to kill and exterminate men, but to cherish and save them.

This simple, modest, and therefore truly
grand figure was not cast in the ready-made
fictitious mould employed by history for the
manufacture of European heroes.

To the valet he is not a great man; the
valet has his own conception of greatness.

XVII.

BERESINA.

THE French troops melted away in a regular mathematical progression.

The passage of the Beresina, concerning which so many volumes have been written, was only one of the intermediate steps in the annihilation of the French army, and not a decisive episode of the campaign.

Much has been written and much will be written about ⸝the passage of the Beresina, because all the single misfortunes which the French army had up to that time endured now accumulated into a mass, and fell upon ⸝them as the bridges broke beneath their feet, leaving in the memory of those who looked on an ineffaceable impression of tragic dis-aster.

The Russians have written volumes about the passage of the Beresina, because Pfühl drew up at St. Petersburg (at that distance from the theatre of war) a plan for drawing Napoleon into a strategical snare on that river. All are persuaded that everything went on conformably to the plan, and they maintain that the passage of the Beresina was the destruction of the French.

Now, the consequences of the passage of the Beresina were less disastrous to the French than was the battle of Krasnoë; they left fewer pieces of artillery and prisoners in the hands of the Russians. Statistics prove this assertion.

The passage of the Beresina served only to prove beyond all doubt the absurdity of the plan for cutting off the retreat of the enemy, and vindicated Koutouzof's idea of simply pursuing the French.

The French hurried on with constantly increasing velocity, concentrating all their energies upon flight. They fled like a wounded animal, and it was impossible to stop them in their course.

The proof of this is what occurred at the bridges, rather than in the arrangements made for the passage.

When the bridges were destroyed, the whole crowd, soldiers without arms, Russian prisoners, women carrying children, all who made up the French train, borne on by the force of inertia, instead of giving themselves up, continued their impetuous course, moving uninterruptedly on, throwing themselves into the boats or falling into the icy waters.

This onward course was reasonable.

The situation of the fugitives and that of the pursuers was equally bad. They press close upon one another in their misfortune, having confidence in their solidarity, and knowing that each has his place with his fellows.

By surrendering to the Russians, their condition, instead of being ameliorated, would have been made worse as far as food and clothing were concerned.

The French did not need exact information to be assured that the Russians did not know what to do with their prisoners, of whom more than half, in spite of their efforts, had died of hunger. The French understood that it could not be otherwise.

The most compassionate generals, those

best disposed toward the French, the French themselves serving in the Russian army, could do nothing for the prisoners, who participated in the misery endured by the Russians.

—The Muscovite generals could not take from their famished soldiers the bread and clothes they needed for the benefit of the French prisoners, however inoffensive and even innocent the latter might be.

There were, however, some Russian generals who favored the prisoners, but they were exceptions.

Behind the French was certain death ; before them, hope. They had burned their bridges, and their only safety was in flight ; and upon this flight they concentrated all their energies.

XVIII.

NAPOLEON AND ALEXANDER I.

IF we agree with the historians that great men lead humanity toward certain ends, such as the greatness of Russia and France, the European balance of power, the propagation of the ideas of the Revolution, progress in general, or any other object, then it is impossible to explain historical events without having recourse to the intervention of accident or of genius.

If the European wars at the beginning of this century had for their object the greatness of Russia, that end might have been attained without the wars and without the invasion.

If, on the contrary, the object in view was the greatness of France, there was no need of the Revolution or of the Empire.

If the proposed end was the propagation of the ideas of the Revolution, books would have accomplished the work better than soldiers.

If, lastly, the progress of civilization was the object, it is sufficiently. evident that there are means for its attainment more efficacious than the destruction of men, and pillage.

Why did events take one course rather than another ? History replies : —

" Accident created the situation and genius profited by it."

But what is " accident," and what is the meaning of the word " genius " ?

" Accident " and " genius " are words which do not represent anything that really exists, and for this reason it is impossible to define them.

They only express a certain way of looking at events.

I am ignorant of the cause of a fact. I believe that I cannot know it, and, accordingly, I do not try to discover it ; I say, it is an accident.

I see that a force has produced an action incompatible with the ordinary qualities of men ; I cannot penetrate to the cause of this force, and I cry, it is genius.

The sheep shut up every night by the

shepherd in a special enclosure, and given
extra food till it becomes twice as fat as
the others, must appear to be a genius to
the rest of the flock. The fact that the
sheep, instead of entering the common fold,
has a place by itself and extra fodder, and,
once fattened, is delivered to the butcher and
killed, doubtless impresses the other sheep
as a result of genius combined with a series
of extraordinary accidents.

But if the sheep stop thinking that everything that goes on is exclusively related to
their own welfare, if they admit that events
may follow ends they cannot comprehend,
they will perceive a unity of action and a
logical conclusion in the fate of the fattened
sheep.

Even if they do not know why it was fattened, they will understand that nothing that
happened to the sheep came by chance, and
they will not be obliged to resort for explanation either to accident or to genius.

Only when we renounce the effort to know
the final end of things, and realize that that
end is wholly beyond our comprehension, do

we discover in the lives of historical personages a logical succession of facts, obedient
to necessity, and then only will be revealed
to us the cause of the disproportion between
their acts and the capacities of ordinary men,
and we shall not be obliged to resort to the
words accident and genius.

Thus, if we admit that the object of the
movements of European peoples is unknown
to us, that we know only certain facts, such as
butcheries in France, then in Prussia, in Austria, and in Russia, and that the cause of
these events must lie in the movement of
the western peoples toward the east, and, inversely, of eastern peoples toward the west, —
admitting this, we no longer have need of
finding genius or anything exceptional in the
character of Napoleon and of Alexander I. ; we
shall see in these personages only men like
other men, we shall have no need of explain-
ing on the score of accident the little events
that made these personages what they were,
and it will be evident to us that these little
events were necessary.

When we give up our search for final ends,

we understand that, just as it is impossible to find on a plant other flowers and other fruits than those which it produces, so is it impossible to imagine two historical personages who, in the place of Alexander I. and Napoleon, would have been able, from the beginning to the end of their lives, to fulfil exactly and in the smallest details the mission that devolved upon them.

The fundamental fact in European events at the beginning of this century is the warlike movements of peoples in mass, first from west to east, and then from east to west.

This movement begins in the west. That the western peoples may have the power to push their warlike advance as far as Moscow, it was necessary : —

1. That they concentrate in a warlike mass of dimensions sufficient to endure the shock of the warlike mass from the east ;

2. That they renounce all their traditions and all their habitudes;

3. That they have at their head, to accomplish this bellicose movement, a man who can justify himself and justify them for resorting to

lies, to pillage, and to massacres, to attain their end.

The little primitive nucleus dating from the French Revolution, not being large enough, disperses. Traditions and habitudes are modified, a new and more considerable group is formed little by little, and with it come new traditions and new habitudes. In this environment the man who is to take his place at the head of the movement and bear all the responsibility of the events that follow is prepared for his mission.

This man, without principles, without habitudes, without traditions, without name, who is not even a Frenchman,—by what seems at first glance a combination of strange and fortuitous circumstances,—glides through all the parties that divide France, and, taking part with none, is placed at the head of all.

The stupidity of those about him, the weakness and inanity of his rivals, his own sincerity in falsehood, and his brilliant and presumptuous egotism, combine to push this man to the head of the army.

The excellent quality of his army in Italy, the

disinclination of the enemy to fight, his confidence in himself and his puerile effrontery, give him military glory.

A multitude of so-called happy accidents meet him everywhere.

The French authorities look at him askance, and their disfavor is useful to him.

The attempts he makes to open a new career fail one after the other; Russia refuses his services, the sultan rejects his offers.

During the war in Italy he is many times within a hair's-breadth of destruction, and always escapes by some unforeseen circumstance.

The Russian troops, the only troops who are able to extinguish his glory, because of manifold diplomatic combinations do not set foot in Europe while he is there.

On his return from Italy he finds the French government in a state of dissolution that must infallibly end in ruin. Napoleon himself devises, as an escape from this dangerous situation, the foolish and haphazard scheme of an expedition to Africa.

Again chance serves him marvellously. Malta, reputed to be impregnable, surrenders be-

fore a shot is fired. Napoleon's most adventur-
ous plans are crowned with success.

The enemy's fleet, which a little later would
not allow the meanest vessel to pass, does not
interfere with the passage of his army.

In Africa, he commits a series of outrages
upon the almost unarmed inhabitants, and the
men who unite with him in these atrocities, and
above all he, their chief, persuade themselves
that what they do is great and noble, that they
are winning glory, and that their exploits are
like those of Cæsar and Alexander of Macedon.

This ideal of *glory* and *greatness*, leading those
who follow it to shrink from no crime and to
surround all their acts with a halo of the super-
natural,— the ideal which is to be the guide
of this man and of all those who join his
fortunes, — grew to enormous proportions in
Africa.

Everything that he undertakes prospers.
The pestilence spares him. Massacre of prisoners is not imputed to him as a crime.

His hurried, puerile, erratic departure, dishon-
orable withal, for he left behind companions in
arms who were in distress, is accounted to him

a meritorious act, and again, the second time, the English fleet allows him to escape.

Then dazzled by the crimes he has committed, and the satisfaction they have brought him, he reaches Paris without any definite object in view. The republican government, which a year before still had the power to put an end to him, is so near dissolution that the presence of this man belonging to no party can only end in his own supremacy.

He has no plan, he fears every one ; but parties see in him their safety, and solicit his support.

For it is he, he alone, with that ideal of glory and greatness built up in Italy and Egypt, with his wild adoration of self, his audacity in crime, his sincerity in falsehood, who is equal to the events which are about to be unfolded.

He is the man needed to occupy the place that waits for him, and so, independently of his own will, without any determined plan, in spite of hesitations and numerous mistakes, he is drawn into a conspiracy which aims at the possession of power, and this conspiracy is crowned with success.

He is thrust into a sitting of the Directory. Alarmed, he wishes to fly, believing himself lost ; he feigns illness, and utters a few foolish words that might have been his destruction.

But the men, once so haughty and determined, who then compose the government of France, feel that their game is over. They are more disturbed than Napoleon, and they say just the contrary of what they should have said to retain their power and overthrow the usurper.

Accident or rather millions of accidents give him power, and all men, as if by agreement, hasten to confirm him in power.

To accident is due the weakness of character which leads the members of the Directory to bow before Napoleon.

Accident makes the character of Paul I., and leads that sovereign to recognize Napoleon's power.

Accident hatches against Napoleon a plot which, instead of destroying, confirms his power.

Through accident the Prince of Enghien comes into his hands, and is assassinated ; and this act, more than any other, proves to the multitude his right, since he possesses the might, to rule.

By accident he gives all his strength to an expedition against England; the enterprise, which would have ruined him, is never carried out, but he falls upon Mack and the Austrian army, and conquers without a battle.

Accident and genius give him the victory at Austerlitz, and, always by accident, all the men of all the nations of all Europe (with the exception of England, which had no part in the events then in progress), all men, in spite of their horror at Napoleon's crimes, recognize his power and his self-assumed title, and regard his ideal of glory and greatness as reasonable and noble.

The forces of the west, as if preparing for a future movement, increase and solidify, after being drawn many times toward the east in 1805, 1806, 1807, and 1809.

By 1811, the group of men formed in France unites with the peoples of Central Europe and forms an enormous mass.

As this mass increases, the man at their

head is proportionately strengthened in his position.

During the ten years of preparation for this great movement, the man has dominated all the sovereigns of Europe. Uncrowned sovereigns have no reasonable ideal to oppose to the foolish ideal of greatness and glory invented by Napoleon. One after another they submit to him, and prove their own insignificance.

The King of Prussia sends his queen to the great man to solicit his good offices ; the Emperor of Austria thinks it will be a favor if the great man will take the daughter of the emperors to his bed ; the pope, guardian of popular holiness, puts religion under the great man's feet.

Napoleon's part is exacted by his environment, which thrusts upon him the responsibility for present and future events, and prepares him for what is to come.

Every act or crime or stroke of luck he essays is received by the world as something heroic.

When the Germans wish to gratify him, they can think of nothing better than celebrations in honor of Jena and Auerstädt.

Greatness is not confined to him ; his ances-
tors, his brothers, his sons-in-law, his brothers-
in-law are also great.

Everything combines to take away his last
vestige of reason, and to prepare him for his
terrible career.

When he is ready, all the forces are also ready.

The invasion rushes toward the east, and
comes to an end at Moscow. The capital is
taken. The Russian army is more thoroughly
shattered than were those of the enemy from
Austerlitz to Wagram.

And now, all of a sudden, in place of the
accidents that have borne him through a series
of uninterrupted successes to the predestined
end, we find in operation an incalculable accu-
mulation of contrary accidents, such as a cold in
the head at Borodino, the sparks that set fire to
Moscow, and the frosts of Russia ; and in place
of genius we discover an incapacity and base-
ness hitherto unknown to history.

The invasion advances backwards, and accident, instead of favoring its progress, turns
against it.

Then we behold an inverse movement, from

east to west, bearing a close resemblance to the preceding movement.

It also is heralded by premonitory activity in 1805, 1807, and 1809. As in the former case, a new group is formed, increases, and becomes a colossal mass. The peoples of central Europe rally to this movement, which is apparently a repetition of the preceding movement, for nothing is wanting to complete the resemblance, neither irresolution midway nor increased velocity as the end draws near.

Paris, the goal of this movement, is reached, and the government of Napoleon and his army is overthrown.

Napoleon himself no longer represents anything. His actions inspire pity and disgust. A new and incomprehensible accident supervenes: the allies hate Napoleon, and regard him as the cause of all their misfortunes.

At this hour, despoiled of his prestige and power, accused of crimes and perfidy, he ought to have been looked upon, as he had been ten years before, or was ten years later, as a bandit, outside of the law; but, by a strange accident, no one considers him in this light.

His part is not yet played to the end. The man who has been declared to be a bandit, outside the law, is sent to an island two days' distance from France, and he is given possession of this island, with a guard, and millions in treasure paid to him. God knows why!

The uprising of peoples begins to abate. The waves fall back, and on the undulations of the sea float a few diplomatists, who imagine that they have brought about the calm.

But the sea rises again. The diplomatists imagine that their dissensions have invoked the storm ; they anticipate another war among their sovereigns. The situation is beyond their control.

But the wave, whose approach they feel, does not come from the direction toward which they are looking.

It is a return of the old wave from the original point of departure, Paris, the last uprising from the west ; an uprising which, all the diplomatists think, will solve all diplomatic difficulties, and put an end to the warlike movement of the period.

The man who has devastated France returns alone, without soldiers, without a plan. He is at the mercy of the guard, but, by a strange accident, no one touches him. On the contrary, every one runs to him in admiration, and receives with acclamations him whom they had cursed the day before, and whom they will curse again a month later. This man is still needed to play his part in the last act.

The act is ended. The play is over. The actor is told to take off his costume and go his way. He is needed no longer.)

For several years more this man plays by himself a pitiable comedy, in solitude at St. Helena. He seeks by lies and intrigues to justify his actions, when justification is no longer necessary.

He shows clearly to the world what a miserable object it was that men took for a force when the invisible hand of Destiny pushed it forward.

The true dispenser of events, having brought the drama to an end, takes away the mask from the principal actor, and reveals his face, saying: "See in whom you have believed! Here he is. You see now that not he, but I, led you."

But, blinded by their prejudices, men have long remained ignorant of the truth.

We find a yet more distinct and inevitable necessity in the life of Alexander I., who was at the head of the counter-movement, from the east toward the west.

What qualities ought a man to possess if he would supplant others and be placed at the head of this movement?

He must have a sentiment of justice, and he must take a real interest, an interest free from all mischievous designs, in the affairs of Europe.

He must have a loftier moral character than that of any other sovereign of his time. He must be gentle and sympathetic. And he must be the victim of outrageous assaults on the part of Napoleon.

All these distinctive traits are found in Alexander I. and have been produced by innumerable accidents, or so-called accidents, in his past life. Everything contributes to this end — his education, his liberal reforms, the counsellors by whom

he is surrounded; we need not include Austerlitz, Tilsit, and Erfurt.

Throughout the duration of the patriotic war,
this personage is inactive, because he is not
needed.

But, as soon as the necessity of a European
war becomes evident, this personage is found at
the critical moment in the place assigned to
him; he is to rally the peoples of Europe and
lead them to the end.

The end is accomplished. After the final
war of 1815, Alexander has at his disposal the
greatest resources of power ever accessible to
man. What use does he make of this power?

Alexander I., the pacificator of Europe, the
man who from his youth had been animated by
a sincere desire to render his peopl ehappy, and
who was the first to grant liberal reforms to his
country, might, we are told, because of his unlimited power, have really established the welfare of his people. What do we see?

While Napoleon, in exile, occupied himself
with lying and puerile plans to show how much
he would do for the good of humanity if only he
had the power, Alexander I., who possesses the

power, having fulfilled his mission, and feeling
the hand of God upon him, realizes, as it were,
at a glance, the nothingness of power, steps
aside, gives himself into the hands of despicable
men, himself capable only of uttering : —

"'Not unto us, O Lord, not unto us, but unto
thy name give glory.' I am a man like other
men. Let me live like a man, that I may think
of my soul and of God."

As the sun or as an atom of the imponderable
ether forms a sphere complete in itself while still
only an atom in the great All inaccessible to
man, so each individual has within himself an
object of existence and at the same time serves
the common object, which is inaccessible to human reason.

A bee, flying from flower to flower, stings a
child, and the child is afraid of bees, declaring
that their object in this world is to sting people.

The poet admires the bee drinking from the
calix of a flower, and assures us that the object
of bees is to breathe the perfume of flowers.

The apiarist sees that the bee gathers pollen
and the juices of plants to nourish the queen

and the larvæ, and he decides that the object of bees is the continuation of their species.

A botanist, observing that the bee bears the fecundating dust from one flower to the pistils of another, assures us that the object of bees is fertilization.

Another botanist, seeing that the transmigration of plants is favored by the bee, declares that the object of the insect is discovered in that mission.

But the real object of the bee is not included in the first or the second or the third, or in any of the objects that the wisdom of man can discover.

The more he seeks to determine this final object, the more evident it is that the object is inaccessible to man.

All he can do is to observe the correlation existing between the life of the bee and the other phenomena of nature.

Man is surrounded by the same limitations, in searching for the final object of events or historical personages; the final object is wholly beyond his reach.

IMPORTANT NEW BOOKS

—PUBLISHED BY—
THOMAS Y. CROWELL & CO., 13 Astor Place, New York.

COUNT TOLSTOI'S WORKS.—The remarkable interest recently awakened by this "great writer of the Russian land" has caused a constantly growing demand for the English translations of his works. The following are now ready:—

ANNA KARÉNINA . . . 12mo, $1.75	MY CONFESSION 12mo, $1.00
CHILDHOOD, BOYHOOD AND YOUTH,	MY RELIGION . . . . . " $1.00
12mo, $1.50	IVAN ILYITCH, &c. . . . " $1.25
THE INVADERS . . . . " $1.25	WHAT TO DO . . . . . " $1.25

A RUSSIAN PROPRIETOR (*in press*).

LES MISÉRABLES.—By VICTOR HUGO. Translated from the French by Isabel F. Hapgood. With 160 full-page illustrations, printed on fine calendered paper, and bound in neat and attractive style. 5 vols., cloth, gilt top, $7.50; half calf, $15.00. Popular edition in one volume, 12mo, $1.50.

The name of the translator is sufficient guaranty that the work has been skilfully and conscientiously performed. It is by far the completest and best translation of this masterpiece. The type is clear and attractive, the illustrations are by famous artists, and the volumes are in every way desirable.

MRS. SHILLABER'S COOK-BOOK.—A Practical Guide for Housekeepers. By Mrs. LYDIA SHILLABER. With an Introduction by Mrs. PARTINGTON. 12mo, cloth, $1.25. Kitchen Edition, in oil-cloth, $1.25. First and second editions sold before publication. Fourth edition now ready.

The connection between laughter and good digestion is proverbial. It is therefore auspicious for the phenomenal success of this sensible and practical work that the genial Mrs. Partington is its sponsor.

TENNYSON'S WORKS.—HANDY VOLUME EDITION. Complete. Large type. From the latest text, including Earlier Poems. Cloth, gilt top, 8 vols., $6.00; parchment, gilt top, $10.50; half calf, gilt edges, $12.00; American seal russia, gilt edge, round corners, $15.00; full calf, flexible, gilt edges, round corners, $21.00; full calf, gilt edges, padded, round corners, $25.00; tree calf, gilt edge, $30.00.

All of the above are boxed in fancy leatherette or calf boxes, according to style of binding, and make the most elegant and convenient edition of this author's poems.

WASHINGTON IRVING'S WORKS.—From new plates. Cloth, 12mo, 6 vols., $7.50; library edition, gilt top, $9.00; half calf, marbled, $15.00.

An admirable library edition of an American classic.

POEMS IN COLOR.—With 56 exquisite illustrations from original designs by W. J. Whittemore.

SEA PICTURES, by Tennyson.	I REMEMBER, by Hood.
SUNRISE ON THE HILLS, by Longfellow.	TO A WATERFOWL, by Bryant.
THE WORSHIP OF NATURE, by Whittier.	TO A MOUNTAIN DAISY, by Burns.

These bright-colored and suggestive little designs are illustrations in the best sense of the word. They interpret the poems. Nothing could be more appropriate for a Christmas or birthday remembrance. 6 volumes. Fancy paper covers, 50 cents each; cloth covers, stamped in gold, 75 cents each; celluloid covers, lithographed, $1.00 each

INITIALS AND PSEUDONYMS.—A Dictionary of Literary Disguises. By WILLIAM CUSHING and ALBERT R. FREY. A new edition, enlarged and revised. Royal, 8vo, cloth, $5.00; half morocco, $7.50; interleaved, cloth, $7.50; interleaved, half morocco, $10.00.

A most convenient and even necessary adjunct for the desk of a literary worker.

CHRIST AND CHRISTIANITY SERIES.—By Rev. H. R. HAWEIS. 5 vols., 12mo, each $1.25.

Those who are familiar with Mr. Haweis's vivid and fascinating style will welcome these five volumes, which are written with deeply religious and earnest feeling.

ST. PAUL'S PROBLEM AND ITS SOLUTION.—Dedicated to the Young People's Society of Christian Endeavor, and setting forth under the guise of fiction the work of this Society. By FAYE HUNTINGTON, author of "Transformed," "What Fide Remembers," etc. 12mo. $1.25.

"It is a good helpful book, whose value and merits can be understood only through a personal reading."—*Church Press.*

SIGRID.—An Icelandic Love Story. Translated from the Danish of JON THORDSSEN THORODDSEN. 12mo. $1.25.

A charming picture of manners and customs in "Ultima Thule."

NEW BOOKS FOR YOUNG PEOPLE

—— PUBLISHED BY ——

THOMAS Y. CROWELL & CO., 13 Astor Place, New York.

FAMOUS AMERICAN AUTHORS. — By SARAH K. BOLTON, author of "Poor Boys Who Became Famous," "Girls Who Became Famous," etc. A series of short biographies, with portraits, of Holmes, Longfellow, Emerson, Lowell, Aldrich, Mark Twain, and other noted writers. 12mo, bevelled boards, $1.50.

Mrs. Bolton has caught the ear of the young, and the latest book from her pen promises to achieve even greater success than its predecessors.

CUORE. — An Italian School-boy's Journal. By EDMONDO DE AMICIS. Translated from the Thirty-ninth Italian Edition, by Isabel F. Hapgood. 12mo. $1.25.

"It has remained for an Italian writer to give to English speaking people the best book for boys that has yet been written. We say this with Tom Brown's delightful schooldays fresh in our recollection." — *Portland Press.*

GIRLS' BOOK OF FAMOUS QUEENS. — By LYDIA HOYT FARMER, author of "Boys' Book of Famous Rulers." Lives of Cleopatra, Queen Elizabeth, Catherine de Medici, Josephine, Victoria, Eugénie, etc. 12mo, cloth. 85 illustrations. $1.50.

"Mrs. Farmer has filled a want never filled before, and met a demand to which there had been no previous reply." — *Boston Traveller.*

BURNHAM BREAKER. — By HOMER GREENE. 12mo. $1.25.

Burnham Breaker is a new and powerful story of the Pennsylvania Coal Regions by the author of the story that won the $1500 prize offered by the *Youth's Companion.*

THE BLIND BROTHER. — ($1500 Prize Volume.) By HOMER GREENE. 12mo, illustrated, 90 cents.

"We know of nothing in recent literature equal to it."

BOYHOOD OF LIVING AUTHORS. — By WILLIAM H. RIDEING. Sketches of the Early Life of Howells, Aldrich, Whittier, Gladstone, Clark Russell, Frank Stockton, etc. 12mo, $1.00.

All the sketches in the volume have been prepared with the consent, and generally with the assistance, of the authors represented. Mainly designed for young readers, it will have, however, an unusual attraction for all who are interested in literary biography.

THE GIANT DWARF. — By J A K 12mo, $1.25. The Giant Dwarf is a simple but eminently sensible and wholesome story of German and American life.

"There is a power of practical suggestion for daily life in these stories that is rather exceptional, and that should give them a household place." — *Boston Traveller.*

WHO SAVED THE SHIP. — By J A K 12mo, $1.25.

"Thoroughly interesting, and free from the taint of sensationalism which mars so much of the juvenile literature of the day." — *Boston Transcript.*

PROFESSOR JOHNNY. — By J A K, author of "Birchwood," "Fitch Club," and "Riverside Museum." 12mo, $1.25.

"An admirable book for teaching boys the science of common things." — *Home Journal.*

FAIRY LEGENDS OF THE FRENCH PROVINCES. — Translated from the original by Mrs. M. CAREY. 12mo, $1.25.

Children of almost any age cannot fail to find perennial pleasure in the racy fancy, shrewd wit, and quaint simplicity of these fascinating tales.

THE ROLLO BOOKS. — By JACOB ABBOTT, "the Prince of Writers for the Young." A new and cheaper edition. 14 vols., bound in 7. Cloth, 16mo, $8.75.

These famous stories, which delighted and instructed the last two generations, seem destined to be no less popular with the young people of the present. Their natural healthiness will always be appreciated by all children.

TWELVE NOTABLE BOOKS.

1. **EMINENT AUTHORS OF THE NINETEENTH CENTURY.** — By Dr. GEORG BRANDES. 12mo. $2.00. A series of essays upon the works of John Stuart Mill, Hans Christian Andersen, Ernest Renan, Gustave Flaubert, and other European writers.
   "The book is one of the most valuable of this decade." — *Traveller.*

2. **THE LABOR MOVEMENT IN AMERICA.** By Professor RICHARD T. ELY. 12mo. $1.50.
   "No one who wishes to understand the problems of labor and capital can afford to be without Professor Ely's work." — *Rochester Chronicle.*
   "The subject has been his specialty for probably a dozen years, and it is safe to say that he is more thoroughly and intimately acquainted with it than any other man in the country." — *Lancaster Intelligencer.*

3. **DEAD SOULS.** By NIKOLAI V. GOGOL. 2 vols. 12mo. $2.50.
   "One of the great novels of this century." — *Beacon.*
   "The work of a thoughtful mind, keen, vigorous, and fertile." — *Nation.*

4. **THE MARQUIS OF PEÑALTA.** By DON ARMANDO PALACIO VALDES. 12mo. $1.50.
   "Any one who wishes to know what Spanish life really is should read 'The Marquis of Peñalta.'"
   "I know of nothing either in ancient or modern novel-writing more natural, charming, attractive, than the graphic narrative of 'The Marquis of Peñalta.'" — *Geo. Parsons Lathrop in the N. Y. Star.*

5. **MEDITATIONS OF A PARISH PRIEST.** By JOSEPH ROUX. 12mo. $1.25.
   "Bright, crisp, incisive, and suggestive." — *Buffalo Express.*
   "Very brilliant, very sagacious, and delightfully unconventional." — *Beacon.*

6. **ST. JOHN'S EVE.** By NIKOLAI V. GOGOL. 12mo. $1.25.
   "Wonderfully fascinating." — *Interior.*
   "The imaginative power and beauty wrought into this story proves Gogol's claim to be an artist in literature." — *Traveller.*

7. **CRIME AND PUNISHMENT.** By FEODOR M. DOSTOYEVSKY. 12mo. $1.50.
   "One of the most moving of modern novels." — *Albany Press.*
   "A book of extraordinary power, a work of genius." — *Christian Union.*

8. **TARAS BULBA.** By NIKOLAI V. GOGOL. 12mo. $1.00.
   "For grandeur, simplicity of conception and superbness of description can hardly be equalled." — *N. Y. Times.*

9. **CHILDHOOD, BOYHOOD, AND YOUTH.** By Count LYOF N. TOLSTOI. 12mo. $1.50.
   "These exquisite sketches belong to the literature which never grows old, which lives forever in the heart of humanity as a cherished revelation." — *Literary World.*

10. **ANNA KARENINA.** By Count LYOF N. TOLSTOI. 12mo. $1.75.
    "Will take rank among the great works of fiction of the age." — *Portland Transcript.*
    "As you read on you say not, 'This is *like* life, but, This *is* life.'" — *W. D. Howells.*

11. **GREAT MASTERS OF RUSSIAN LITERATURE.** By M. ERNEST DUPUY. 12mo. $1.25.
    "This volume, with its clear outlines of the lives and works of Gogol, Turgenief, and Tolstoi, will be found a most available and useful hand-book." — *Traveller.*

12. **MY RELIGION.** By Count LYOF N. TOLSTOI. 12mo. $1.00.
    "A book which should go to every household where the New Testament is read." — *N. Y. Sun.*

THOMAS Y. CROWELL & CO., 13 Astor Place, New York.

Books of Permanent Worth and Enduring Value.

ROGET'S THESAURUS OF ENGLISH WORDS AND PHRASES. Classified and arranged so as to facilitate the expression of ideas and assist in literary composition. NEW EDITION. Revised and enlarged by the author's son, J. L. Roget. Crown 8vo, cloth extra, $2.00.

A DICTIONARY OF QUOTATIONS FROM THE POETS. Based upon that of Henry G. Bohn. Revised, corrected, and enlarged by the addition of over 1200 quotations. With index of authors, chronological data, and concordance index. By ANNA L. WARD. Introductory preface by R. H. STODDARD. Crown 8vo, bevelled boards, cloth, $2.50; interleaved edition, cloth, $3.50; half calf or half morocco, $5.00.
"The more competent the critic who examines it, the heartier will be his favorable verdict." — *Congregationalist.*

INITIALS AND PSEUDONYMS. A Dictionary of Literary Disguises. By WILLIAM CUSHING, A.M. Giving the *noms de plume* and real names of nearly 7,000 authors, with brief notices, date of writer's birth and death, etc. Royal 8vo, cloth, $5 00; half morocco, $7.50.
"A book for which every man of letters will be grateful. Of inestimable value to literary students and journalists, and ought to be in every library in the world." — *N. Y. Mail and Express.*

CAMBRIDGE BOOK OF POETRY AND SONG. Selected from English and American authors. Collected and edited by CHARLOTTE F. BATES, of Cambridge, compiler of "The Longfellow Birthday Book," "Seven Voices of Sympathy," etc. With a steel portrait of Longfellow, and 16 full-page illustrations, from original designs. Royal 8vo, cloth, gilt edges, $5.00; half moroc., gilt, $7.50; full moroc., gilt, $10.00; tree calf, gilt, $12.00.
"Eminently useful as a book of reference for those who write and those who are making a special study of poetical literature." — *Boston Transcript.*

TENNYSON'S POEMS. A New and Complete Edition. Illustrated by CHURCH, DIELMAN, SCHELL, HARRY FENN, and other artists. With portrait, 24 full-page illustrations, and vignette titles, engraved by Andrew. Uniform in style with the Cambridge Book of Poetry. The finest edition of Tennyson ever published in this country. Royal 8vo, cloth, gilt, $5 00; morocco, $10.00; tree calf, $12.00.
"One of the most superb books of any time." — *News, Indianapolis.*

HER MAJESTY'S TOWER. By W. HEPWORTH DIXON. A History of the Tower of London. From the seventh London edition. 2 vols. 12mo, with 47 illustrations, $3.50; half calf, $7.50.
"The most complete story of this historic structure there is in existence." — *Hartford Post.*

PRINCES, AUTHORS AND STATESMEN OF OUR TIME. By Canon Farrar, James T. Fields, and other popular writers. Edited by James Parton. Sixty illustrations, 1 vol., 8vo, cloth, $2.75.
"The high character of the writers is a guaranty of its general excellence and trustworthiness." — *Detroit Post.*

MULLER'S LIFE OF TRUST. With an introduction by Francis Wayland. New Edition. Enlarged and illustrated. 12mo. $1.50.

LIFE AND EPISTLES OF SAINT PAUL. By Conybeare and Howson. With maps and illustrations. 12mo. $1.50; cheap edition, without illustrations, $1.00.
"A marvel of Scripture Biography." — *Spurgeon.*

GEORGE ELIOT'S POEMS. Illustrated edition, with 16 full-page illustrations by Garrett, St. John Harper, and others. Engraved by Geo. T. Andrew. 8vo, cloth, full gilt, $4.50; full morocco, $9.00; tree calf, $9.00.
"Nothing better need be asked for in the form of a presentation book." — *Providence Journal.*

RED LETTER POEMS. By English men and women from Chaucer down to the present day. Illustrated edition with 24 illustrations, 8vo, cloth, $2.50; full morocco or tree calf, $6.00.
"By far the best collection of English Poetry ever made." — *H. T. Suddurt — Ohio University.*

THOMAS Y. CROWELL & CO., 13 Astor Place, New York.